FREEDOM
from
FEAR

OTHER BOOKS BY FORREST CHURCH

Father and Son

The Devil and Dr. Church

Entertaining Angels

The Seven Deadly Virtues

Everyday Miracles

A Chosen Faith
(with John A. Buehrens)

God and Other Famous Liberals

Life Lines

Lifecraft

Bringing God Home

The American Creed

FREEDOM
from
FEAR

*Finding the Courage
to Act, Love, and Be*

FORREST CHURCH

ST. MARTIN'S PRESS   NEW YORK

www.stmartins.com

Design by Phil Mazzone

Library of Congress Cataloging-in-Publication Data

Church, F. Forrest.
    Freedom from fear : finding the courage to act, love, and be / Forrest Church.
        p. cm.
    ISBN 0-312-32533-9
    EAN 978-0312-32533-6
    1. Fear—Religious aspects—Christianity. I. Title.

BV4908.5.C42 2004
241'.4—dc22

                                                    2003070882

First Edition: July 2004

10 9 8 7 6 5 4 3 2 1

To the All Souls family in New York City, whom I have been honored to serve for more than a quarter century. I disguise several of you in the retelling of your stories, but you know who you are and how much you have taught me.

The only thing we have to fear is fear itself.

—Franklin Delano Roosevelt,
March 4, 1933

CONTENTS

Introduction xiii

FEAR

  Fear Itself 3
  The Five Fears 9
  Fright 17
  Worry 23
  Guilt 31
  Insecurity 39
  Dread 45

COURAGE

  Three Kinds of Courage .53
  The Courage to Act 59
  The Courage to Love 67
  The Courage to Be 77

FREEDOM

  Ten Keys to Freedom—Lightening Up 85
  Practicing Thoughtful Wishing 89
  Resetting Our Alarms 93

Posting a "No Vacancy" Sign 101
Unwrapping the Present 107
Taking the Stage 115
Acting on 60 Percent Convictions 121
Remembering the Secret to It All 127
Praying for the Right Miracle 135
Letting Go for Dear Life 139

THE *FREEDOM FROM FEAR* BOOK CLUB

Resources for Courage 149

Classics in Courage

To Kill a Mockingbird Harper Lee 153
Robinson Crusoe Daniel Defoe 161
The Little Prince Antoine de Saint-Exupéry 169

Seven Fear Experts

The Gift of Fear Gavin de Becker 177
From Panic to Power Lucinda Bassett 181
The Answer to How Is Yes Peter Block 185
Freeing the Soul from Fear Robert Sardello 189
Embracing Fear Thom Rutledge 193
Feel the Fear and Do It Anyway Susan Jeffers 197
Love Is Letting Go of Fear Gerald G. Jampolsky ...201

Freedom from Fear Study Guide 205

Acknowledgments 209

INTRODUCTION

Her eyes told me everything. Within the minute it took for her to enter my study, sit down on the couch, and arrange the notes she had scribbled to herself on little scraps of paper, the fear her eyes conveyed spoke volumes. I could easily imagine how she procrastinated for days before making the appointment, then almost called to cancel at the last minute, and now wished that she had. The first thing she confessed to, even before greeting me, was embarrassment. As people in real trouble often do, she apologized for wasting my "precious time on something so trivial." Beyond these telling words, her body language, too, revealed deep feelings of inadequacy. And also apprehension, perhaps that I might judge her as severely as she judged herself, or let her down somehow. And yet by the end of that long, fear-packed minute, I began to sense something else—how relieved she was at last to be unburdening herself of a weight she could no longer carry.

Over the past three decades, I have spent thousands of pastoral counseling hours helping people unload their fears. I am a minister, not a therapist. Rather than listen and work patiently over a protracted period, I tend to meet with people only once or twice, as I did with this young woman. Time being of the essence, we got right down to business. She had come seeking practical advice, so I tried to offer nuggets of wisdom that she could take home and put right to the test. Fear lies at the center of so many of our troubles. As were the thoughts I offered her, much of my advice is therefore aimed at stimulating courage: the courage to act, the courage to love, and the courage to be.

Judging from my counseling sessions over the past two years, fear's grip is tightening. Never have I encountered a higher general fear level. It extends across all ranks: children and retirees; couples and individuals; the unemployed and professionals at the peak of their careers and earning potential, flush with health and blessed with wonderful families. That fear should flourish where we might least expect it should not surprise us. Like a drop of iodine in a glass of water, fear that might strike an outsider as trivial can color an entire life.

Some fears affect almost everyone. Surely 9/11 is responsible for fear's heightened presence among us, but other factors are at work as well. An unpredictable economy affects our sense of future security, as do rapid cultural and geopolitical change. Fear thrives on uncertainty. With knowledge multiplying faster than wisdom, we live in uncertain times. And fear is contagious—we catch it from one another. Even if we didn't, it would spring up on its own. To fear is human: it comes with the territory. So if you find yourself unsettled by your fears, don't feel alone.

I said this to the fearful young woman sitting across from me—"Don't feel alone." I also told her she would be all right. If she comes to believe this, she almost surely will be all right. (Her fears had to do with an unresolved personal relationship. I had no idea whether *it* could be made right, only that *she* could, as long as she framed her thoughts and directed her actions in a courageous, positive way.) But fear is a persuasive advocate. It does everything possible to turn each of us into the Little Engine That Couldn't.

Over the years, I have discovered that fear has a logic (or an illogic) all its own. This woman feared getting married *and* remaining single. Others of us fear illness *and* doctors, or being isolated at home *and* being trapped in a crowd. Many of us manage to fear both failure *and* success. Such confusion extends across fear's spectrum, culminating in the fear of death—which leads directly to a fear of life. Afraid to die, we fear to live, because life is dangerous.

In fact, life is fatal. Attempts to eliminate risk ultimately fail. To the extent that we do eliminate risk from life, we may also succeed in sucking the air out of it. "A ship in the harbor is safe, but that is not what ships are built for," a wise observer said. Those of us who prove most successful at protecting ourselves from harm eventually discover (or, even more sadly, fail to discover) that absolute security and complete safety are perfect synonyms for death.

To bring ourselves to life requires courage. We might begin with a greater appreciation for the courage we already possess. Motherhood produces millions of heroes every day. So do marriage and living alone, friendship, work, illness, loss, and the many other conditions in which we find ourselves. Yet, like the woman who walked through her fear into my study, when frightened we feel anything but courageous. We forget that courage shines only in fear's shadow. John Wayne put it simply: "Courage is being scared to death—and saddling up anyway."

Fear doesn't only exist within us. It permeates the very institutions that contain our lives. Every one of them, from the family to the corporation, has a built-in hierarchy of fear. Students fear their teachers, workers their bosses, children their parents, patients their doctors. When there is no equality in a marriage, wives fear their husbands (or husbands their wives).

Even with our peers, beginning with our siblings, we live in a world structured by competition and therefore built on a foundation of fear. We encounter it whenever we are evaluated, contrasted with others, or asked to perform—and this means almost constantly (for grades, favors, dates, jobs, promotions, raises, and to keep up with the neighbors). Fear thrives on comparison. In each contest we enter, we risk the stigma of losing or being deemed unacceptable. From home to work and back again, fear is institutionalized in almost all the places we inhabit. No wonder we feel it so often.

Fear has its own hierarchy of sorts. After a lifetime of observation—in the laboratory of my study, brainstorming together with one co-researcher at a time—I have broken fear down into five basic types, associated respectively with the body, intellect, conscience, emotions, and soul:

1. **Fright** is instinctive fear, designed to protect us from physical danger.

2. **Worry** is fear produced by our worst imaginings.

3. **Guilt** is fear caused by a troubled conscience.

4. **Insecurity** is fear prompted by feelings of inadequacy.

5. **Dread** is fear generated by life's fundamental uncertainty.

I have also come to recognize three distinct kinds of courage, defined, in this case, according to their objective. We require:

1. **The courage to act**—because performing is a gutsy thing to do.

2. **The courage to love**—because open hearts break easily.

3. **The courage to be**—because, all by itself, life can be frightening.

Winston Churchill considered courage the greatest of all virtues, since we can't exhibit the others without it. If we lack the courage to act (or to control our actions), justice, temperance, and prudence are impossible. Without the courage to love, love can never be sustained. Nor can faith or hope flourish apart from the courage to be.

All three kinds of courage require heart. It is no accident that the two words (the French *coeur,* or "heart," and the English *courage*) are so closely related. Courage is when fear speaks and the heart answers. After absorbing fear's best argument, the heart says no. Nothing out of the ordinary is required. There is no secret password, no special formula. Anyone, and at almost any time, can find the courage to answer fear. The woman I counseled could, and so can you. In fact, the wisdom that makes courage possible is so universal and elemental that I can sum it up in three short imperatives:

1. Do what you can.

2. Want what you have.

3. Be who you are.

It is that simple. And also that difficult.

Freedom from Fear rests on the proposition that fear and freedom are opposites, a life ruled by fear cannot be free, and courage can liberate our lives from fear's reign. I open by examining fear itself, describing each of the five fears in some detail. I then turn to courage, taking much the same approach to the three kinds of courage. The heart of the book—ten keys to freedom—reveals how, armed with courage, we can employ ten useful devices to free our lives from fear:

1. Lightening Up

2. Practicing Thoughtful Wishing

3. Resetting Our Alarms

4. Posting a "No Vacancy" Sign

5. Unwrapping the Present

6. Taking the Stage

7. Acting on 60 Percent Convictions

8. Remembering the Secret to It All

9. Praying for the Right Miracle

10. Letting Go for Dear Life

Paying attention to these ten principles, individually and taken together, will lead to the self-acceptance, integrity, and gratitude essential for freedom from fear.

To deepen our discussion, the *Freedom from Fear* Book Club features ten books, each addressing fundamental questions pertaining to fear and courage. First, I introduce *To Kill a Mockingbird, Robinson Crusoe,* and *The Little Prince,* because these familiar classics offer inspirational lessons that illustrate the principles in *Freedom from Fear* uncommonly well. Following these introductions are summaries of books written by seven thoughtful men and women who have devoted much of their careers to the study of fear. I close with a brief study guide for this book designed to facilitate individual reflection or group discussion.

My goal throughout is the same as it was when that fearful young woman walked into my study and sat down for an hour's conversation. We shall spend what I hope will be a little quality time together searching for the courage to act, love, and be.

FEAR

FEAR ITSELF

Franklin Delano Roosevelt suggested the title of this book. He also did as much as anyone I can think of to counter the power of "fear itself."

It was a cold, late winter's Saturday, the sky a canopy of gray clouds, matching the spirit of the times. When a hundred thousand Americans gathered on March 4, 1933, to hear the new president—a crowd extending from the steps of Washington's Capitol far into the distance around the reflecting pool and down the great mall—times were darker than they are today. Near the bottom of the deepest depression in its history, America had fallen precipitously from the high-stepping days of the Roaring Twenties. The boom had gone bust, one quarter of the population could find no work, soup lines wound around entire city blocks, and shantytowns turned parks into slums. Yesterday's rich young men, if not actually jumping from Wall Street office windows, were cast into bankruptcy. People turned against their neighbors, looking for scapegoats, driven to violence by desperation. The government appeared paralyzed, and indeed nothing Washington tried seemed to work. The whole fabric of society was unraveling before a helpless nation's very eyes.

Though he had shown little beyond an honorable yet unspectacular public career to indicate he had the stuff to reverse the nation's fortunes, Franklin Delano Roosevelt put his finger on the problem. He didn't talk about how the government could work with business and labor to lift us out of the Depression, or propose any radical social or economic program; the New Deal would come later. What the new president did was to utter the hitherto unspoken word that lurked in everyone's heart—*fear*. "The only thing we have to fear is fear itself," he said.

No other presidential address matches Roosevelt's First Inaugural in the directness and immediacy of its impact. At the end of the speech, witnesses say, the applause was thunderous, rolling like waves. The president clapped in rhythm with the crowd. To the millions more listening on radio, the effect was even greater, more intimately felt, almost personal, as if he were speaking to each American individually. Any speech can be heard. This one the audience actually lived. Our president's confidence became the nation's own.

In the morning papers, the press—hardened and skeptical then as today—reflected the relief and exultation of a weary people. Even pundits who faulted the text on political grounds applauded its tone. "No more vital utterance was ever made by a president of the United States," read an editorial in the *Atlanta Constitution*. "Confidence literally arose from its hiding place and is today a living reality," another journalist wrote.

For all of that, we can't credit Roosevelt with originality. Centuries before, in his *Essays*, Montaigne had confessed: "The thing I fear most is fear." Lord Wellington, victor over Napoleon at Waterloo, called fear "the only thing I am afraid of." Henry David Thoreau said much the same thing:

"Nothing is so much to be feared as fear." But by saying what he did when he did and in the way he did, Roosevelt gave heart to an entire country.

I serve on the board of the Franklin and Eleanor Roosevelt Institute, a not-for-profit foundation dedicated to the Roosevelt legacy. Among my duties, I chair the committee that presents the Roosevelt Four Freedoms Medals to men and women whose distinguished service carries forward the Roosevelt spirit. The Four Freedoms Medals hearken back to FDR's second immortal speech, his Annual Address to Congress delivered on January 6, 1941, familiarly known as the Four Freedoms Address. In it he proclaimed four basic freedoms—freedom of speech, freedom of worship, freedom from want, and freedom from fear. These freedoms demand our protection and extension "everywhere in the world," he said. Just months before the nation's entry into World War II, that President Roosevelt should include a new freedom—freedom from fear—among those essential to humanity is significant. With fear again the heart's unspoken watchword, he echoed his reminder that fear itself constitutes a fundamental danger to human existence. By adding this new freedom to others familiar in American history, he elevated freedom from fear to the founders' altar.

Whether with respect to us as a nation or as individuals, the promise of human freedom is denied to anyone living under the tyranny of fear. My focus here is on personal rather than civic freedom, although the two certainly overlap. Roosevelt's own story demonstrates how. His unassailable confidence heartened the nation, but he learned courage on his own, when in 1921, at the age of thirty-nine, he was struck by polio (or, perhaps, a recent study suggests, by Guilliame Barre syndrome). Paralyzed from the waist down, Roosevelt lay bedridden for half a year, his ambitions suspended in a newly uncertain future.

Shortly before she died, his mother, Sara, confessed that he had never spoken to her directly about his medical condition. When she first saw him in his crippled state, Sara made this report in a letter to her brother:

> I got here yesterday at 1:30 and at once . . . came up to a brave, smiling, and beautiful son, who said: "Well, I'm glad you are back, Mummy, and I got up this party for you!" He had shaved himself and seems very bright and keen. Below his waist he cannot move at all. His legs (that I have always been proud of) have to be moved often as they ache when long in one position. He and Eleanor decided at once to be cheerful and the atmosphere of the house is all happiness, so I have fallen in and follow their glorious example.

This is precisely what the American people were to do, both during the Great Depression and World War II: they fell in and followed FDR's glorious example. Though he could not walk without support, often relying on his sons to accompany him on painstaking journeys from dais to podium, it was impossible to think of this man as an invalid. He did disguise the fact, abetted by gracious opponents and a sympathetic press corps. Yet most Americans perceived their leader to be fitter than he appeared. Almost everybody believed he had fully recovered from his "bout" with polio.

One reason for this belief is that Roosevelt practiced what he preached, maintaining an almost magical serenity. In seminary, ministerial candidates are taught the importance of being a "non-anxious" presence for their congregations. Roosevelt was a non-anxious presence for the entire nation, beginning with his closest associates and extending over the radio in his fireside chats to all Americans in the intimacy of their living rooms.

His detractors (and there were many) found him insufferably arrogant. *Cocksure, impudent,* and *presumptuous* are among the gentler adjectives employed by his enemies in colorful defamation of Roosevelt's character. People who loved him saw instead a dashing bon vivant with a will of iron. The words that jump to my mind when I think of Franklin Roosevelt—*jauntiness, spirit, faith, self-assurance, effervescence, courage, confidence, mettle,* and *aplomb*—can all be listed among fear's antonyms. The one word you never hear associated with Franklin Delano Roosevelt, by friend or foe alike, is *fear.*

Yet think of all he was up against. The times in which he lived and led were, on balance, more trying than our own. He could not dress himself without assistance and was never without pain. He devoted the better part of a decade (throughout his early forties) to a single-minded effort to walk again and failed almost completely. But he was never defeated. How much finer this is than to be defeated without failing, which happens whenever we refuse to try.

It is not the least bit surprising that of Roosevelt's many fine speeches, the two that history prizes most highly address the subject of fear, for he considered fear itself to be the greatest enemy of a free people. Psychologically, he knew, fear is more paralyzing than polio, more depressing than the greatest depression, and as crippling as war.

In our personal lives as well, fear and freedom are opposites; each casts the other out. For freedom to displace fear from its lodging in our heart, it is essential for us to remember who the real enemy is—fear itself.

THE FIVE FEARS

Franklin Roosevelt advocated freedom from worry and dread, not freedom from safety or from a guilty conscience. Keeping our fears straight is important, because fears such as fright or guilt can be beneficial. Even if it were possible, which it is not, freedom from *all* fear would be harmful to both body and soul.

Over the years, I have come to recognize five underlying types of fear. My categories are not scientific, but experience confirms them and I know that they serve a practical purpose. Fear comes in a wide array of sizes as well, ranging from trivial fretfulness to outright panic. In extreme instances, every type of fear can trigger panic, and each finds muted expression in fretfulness.

Any attempt to divide fear neatly into a set of subgroupings is further complicated by its vast vocabulary. One indication of how prevalent a role fear plays in our lives is that there are almost as many synonyms for it as there are Aleut words for snow: *terror, horror, apprehension, trepidation, perturbation, foreboding, concern, angst, agitation, anxiety,*

consternation, dread, fright, worry, cowardice, fainthearted-
ness, chickenheartedness, disquiet, guilt, temerity, dismay,
and *alarm.* Surely there are more. Yet almost none of these
words describes a single type of fear so perfectly that it
couldn't double for another. This is one reason most fear experts distinguish more broadly—between fears that are
helpful and harmful, or real and imaginary (a distinction
that has its own problems, because the fear is real, even
when its cause is imaginary). Nonetheless, I find separating
fear into five basic classes helpful. Here is a thumbnail
sketch of each.

FRIGHT (FEAR CENTERED IN THE BODY)

Fright triggers the body's response to physical danger. Innate and reflexive, it is the one fear for which we should all
be thankful. It may even save our lives.

I am driving down Highway 80 in New Jersey one twilit
evening on my way to visit my son at school. Surfing channels on the radio, I let my attention stray for just a moment.
When I return my eyes to the road before me, it has van-
ished without a trace. In its stead, filling the windshield of
my suddenly tiny automobile, is the stark, looming back of a
huge semitrailer, my car seconds away from catastrophic
impact. Fear seizes my entire body. Time freezes into slow-
motion frames. In a dreamlike sequence, my car brakes,
skids, spins, screeches, and banks to a stop on the shoulder—
my fear has commandeered my actions and brought me to
safety.

Science can now elucidate how fear made the blood rush
to my head—and with it, heightened consciousness—by re-
leasing a surge of adrenaline that brought even the tiny
hairs along my spine to attention. It can explain why my

mouth fell open (so I could yell if I needed to) and my eyes bugged out (to record information as quickly as possible). It can give me the physiological reasons why, once safe on the shoulder of the road, I poured sweat and gasped for air. Scientists can tell me how, from the tiny amygdala headquartered in my brain, millions of fear soldiers rushed to the battlements and rescued me—or perhaps more exactly, helped me rescue myself.

Not that such a production is always necessary. Fright is a vestige from our distant ancestry, when fear was our constant companion. Today it makes us jump more often than we need to. In fact, we can mark human progress by how many more false alarms we experience than our forebears did.

One feature differentiates fright from the other forms of fear. It takes place completely in the present rather than visiting from the future, where imagined dangers lurk. As brief as it is intense, fright works on a hair trigger. Other forms of fear may linger after a physical scare, thereby appearing to be extensions of fright, but direct, instinctive, physical fear passes with the danger, whether that danger is perceived or real.

WORRY (FEAR CENTERED IN THE INTELLECT)

Any fear that recurs or malingers is more likely to pose a danger than protect us from one. This is certainly the case with worry, a word we might safely define as "apprehension about things that are unlikely to take place." Shortly before his death, Mark Twain mused, "I am an old man and have known a great many troubles, but most of them never happened."

Driven by the imagination, worry directs our thoughts to things that might occur to endanger or diminish our lives.

Bad things do happen to us; the problem with worry is how indiscriminate it is. Worry is also debilitating, overwhelming us to the point that, on those occasions when the object of our concern does actually pose a threat to our well-being, we are paralyzed from taking reasonable steps to defuse it. One woman can spend a year worrying about whether she has cancer before going to the doctor to find out either that she doesn't or that it is now too late to do anything about it. Another woman can worry so much about telltale signs of aging that she fails to enjoy her youth.

"Worry represents the interest we pay on trouble before it comes due," a wit once quipped. Remember the Y2K epidemic? Most computers were preset to revert to 1900 when the year 2000 rolled around, potentially creating economic chaos. This was a real problem, one that required not denial or escape but serious attention. Yet initially the worry was compounded, as fear often is, by procrastination. Though a fixed and unavoidable deadline loomed, panic and paralysis prevailed in many businesses. But legitimate concern soon meshed all the spinning wheels into concerted action. Technicians were hired to address the problem. Before long these experts were too busy fixing it to worry away any of their precious energy. That sacrifice was set aside for the rest of us, the millions of bystanders who, apart from drawing down our bank accounts and putting our savings under the mattress, could do nothing but worry. Public opinion polls taken at the time concluded that in the United States alone, 70 million of us believed that we would be directly affected by the Y2K problem. As if inspired by Pan, the mischievous god of panic, fear had a field day. Yet this crisis did not—any more than the advent of a new millennium—represent the end of the world. As with many legitimate worries, met squarely it could be neutralized, and so it was.

GUILT (FEAR CENTERED IN THE CONSCIENCE)

Guilt is the most evenhanded of fears. On the one hand, our conscience can paralyze us for no good reason; on the other, it can force us to change our lives for the better.

When we have done something truly bad, guilt—though often first expressed as the fear of getting caught—works on behalf of our better self. On such occasions, not only do we deserve conscience's pangs and the fear that accompanies them, but such fear can also awaken us to moral opportunity. Guilt can prompt us to undertake a thorough moral inventory and housecleaning.

Many of us are more familiar with guilt's dysfunctional twin. When our conscience becomes hyperactive (as a kind of moral lint collector), guilt commandeers our entire existence. Such fear is as crippling as it is unnecessary. We examine and cross-examine our every little act so mercilessly that we can finally do no right.

Being human, we err. Some call this original sin; it certainly suggests original guilt and demands the rites of self-acceptance and forgiveness. A moral perfectionist lives in constant fear because moral perfection lies beyond our grasp. Perfectionism is a form of self-abuse. When we impose on others the same impossible set of standards that we inflict on ourselves, we jeopardize everyone's happiness. It is therefore important to discriminate between good and bad guilt. We need to lighten up but not take ourselves off the moral hook. As long as we continue to tolerate our bad behavior—if our conscience is in any kind of working order—guilt will rightly haunt us.

In Judaism, Christianity, and Islam, guilt finds its quintessential expression in "the fear of God." Deeming God to be all-knowing and all-powerful, the ultimate authority and final judge, the believer fears being brought up on charges before the divine tribunal. Not every action prompted by this fear is justified. Overly sensitive souls may cower under the bedcovers when they could just as innocently be playing outdoors. When called for, however, guilt nags at our conscience until we finally fess up, make reparations, go and sin no longer. Confucius put it simply: "When you have moral faults, do not fear to abandon them."

INSECURITY (FEAR CENTERED IN THE EMOTIONS)

If fright is triggered by danger, worry by imagination, and guilt by conscience, insecurity almost always comes packaged with inadequacy. Insecurity is a form of narcissism. Being self-conscious, we are less conscious of others. For the same reason, we stand apart or feel apart, even in a crowd. With perfect one-way X-ray vision, we feel conspicuous in a world filled with people who appear to know exactly how to dress for life's every occasion. When fraught by feelings of inadequacy, we want nothing more than simply to disappear. Success and failure, public speaking, crowds, the telephone, and authorities: these things, among many others, trigger insecurity and leave us scurrying for cover.

As a rule, we are less quick to pursue pleasure than to run from pain. Since with each new human encounter we risk embarrassment, those of us who suffer from acute insecurity do only those things that will guarantee our emotional safety. Putting fear in charge of our agenda, we venture out into the world ever more tentatively. We always have a good excuse, some version of "It might rain." We languish in private gardens, with walls so high that nothing can grow there.

Emotional deprivation is the price we pay for avoiding emotional vulnerability. Fearing that we may spill life's precious cup, we lift it ever more cautiously to our lips, and slowly its contents evaporate. Since fighting feelings of inadequacy exacerbates them and running away buries them deeper in the psyche, there is only one sure solution to this dilemma—transcending it. We empty our cup and are filled. Our cup runneth over.

DREAD (FEAR CENTERED IN THE SOUL)

Dread and anxiety distinguish themselves from all other fears by having no fixed object. They grasp at whatever straws may be available. Anxiety is driven by a sense of not being in control of our life and destiny, and dread is anxiety's darkest expression. The two are related in the same way that the tenor and bass clefs are related in music: anxiety tends to be high-pitched and nervous; dread is somber. When anxiety intensifies into what is popularly known as "anxiety disorder," it can lead to a complete meltdown, like the story about the tiger that chases its tail around a tree until it turns into a pool of butter. Dread, however, draws us down toward the abyss.

Normal anxiety manifests itself in each of the other forms of fear (fright, guilt, worry, and insecurity). When anxious, we are jumpy and therefore subject to fright. Caught up in anxiety's undiscriminating dither, we may also morph into guilt-ridden, insecure worrywarts. To regain equilibrium, we need to compartmentalize our anxiety into its constituent parts and remove their hooks one by one.

Dread presents a different kind of challenge. The most philosophical of fears, it arises from the recognition that life will one day annihilate us. I might best describe it as an allergic reaction to life, kind of a spiritual asthma. Anyone with asthma—I have a mild form—knows that its severity grows in proportion to the extent that we try to control it. With each forced breath, the lungs constrict. Serious asthma spurs legitimate concern and demands medical vigilance, but in mild cases often all it takes for an attack to subside is to stop obsessing over it. Watch a television show. Read a book. Dread works in much the same way. We can loosen its grip by focusing our attention elsewhere.

"Man himself produces dread," wrote the Christian philosopher Søren Kierkegaard. We manufacture it whenever we attempt to control things over which we hold no final authority. We reduce life to a battleground, where we struggle against insurmountable odds. Fearing every transition from certainty to uncertainty, we devote our full energy to protecting ourselves against loss. Dread is the opposite of trust. The more we dread death and dying, the more alarming life and living turn out to be.

These, then—fright, worry, guilt, insecurity, and dread— are the five fears. When fear forces us off the highway to avoid getting killed or conspires with our conscience to prompt needed changes in our lives, we are right to welcome its alarms. But when it misdirects us down long, unnecessary detours, detracting from our journey without making it any safer, the time has come to pull over and ask for directions.

FRIGHT

From birth, we are hardwired to be frightened of two things—loud noises and falling. Most of the other things that frighten us are learned. Either people teach us later that we should fear this monster or that, or we learn to be scared on our own from hard experience. The old song from *South Pacific* reminds us that "hate must be carefully taught." Fear, too, must be taught carefully, for if we are not careful, we shall end up frightened of everything. But not all fear must be taught. Some fear comes with the territory. We are born with it.

Of the fears we are born with, the fear of falling suggests perceived immediate danger, and loud noises might be expanded to include anything that startles us. On certain terrifying occasions—such as when a plane hits an air pocket and drops hundreds of feet in a matter of seconds—these two innate fears double up.

Contrast our physical response on such an occasion to the fear of flying itself. However irrational, to anyone who experiences it, the fear of flying is no less real. Even the

Dalai Lama is afraid of flying. Yet, apart from the pope, the Dalai Lama has probably flown more places on this earth than almost anyone else. Over time he has learned fear's most important lesson: those who muster the courage to do things that scare them master their fear. These days, the Dalai Lama reports, only rarely do his knuckles get white when he flies. He has slowly built up a tolerance for flying and, with that tolerance, a growth in trust. "The more I fly," he says, "the less I sweat."

Such progress can't be measured in the case of sudden fright. The same startling thing can happen a hundred times and we remain as susceptible as the very first time terror struck. I'm told that even the most experienced pilots feel a catch in their stomachs when their planes hit an air pocket.

The fact that spontaneous fright is not learned but instinctive doesn't mean it always hits the mark. Some things that take us by surprise turn out to be bogeymen. One morning I was sitting in my office, rapt in concentration, pondering how I might best continue this chapter. A coworker walked in without my noticing and approached me from behind. When she tapped me on the shoulder, I must have jumped a full inch, scared out of my skin. In one of those mini–chain reactions so typical of fear, the instant I jumped, she recoiled in alarm. We both caught our breath, laughed for a second or two, and then got on with our business as if nothing had happened. But something *had* happened. She frightened me almost to death. Quicker than those tiny histamines that swarm to counter the poison of an insect bite—leaving a nettlesome, itchy bump as a monument to overvigilance—the fear brigade, at the slightest registered hint of danger, managed to ring almost every alarm in my body. I tried to appear unruffled, but it took at least a minute for me to redeploy my emergency fear SWAT team back to its barracks in the recesses of the mind.

Even when we put our fear police to bed, they do not sleep. They stand silent sentry, protecting us from real and imagined harm. They even monitor our dreams. We can count on them to be there for us when we don't need them—and when we really do.

We all know the physical symptoms of fear. They are the same whether we are startled by a tap on the shoulder or almost killed on the highway. Chests tighten; mouths parch; throats clench. Sometimes we have to stop and catch our breath, and our muscles may feel suddenly weak. Scientists once had a straightforward view of how these symptoms were triggered. They imagined the brain as a processing shop of linear sensory data, much like an assembly line. First we take in data from our eyes and ears and send it to the thinking and reasoning part of the brain, the cerebral cortex. The cerebral cortex then breaks down the data, organizes it, and distributes signals to the body to act in accordance with its instructions. Today brain researchers have discovered that both emotional and physical reactions to external stimuli are channeled through a much more complex circuitry. The cerebral cortex is not the only driver of our fear response system. One pioneer of the new model by which we understand how the brain works, Columbia University scientist David Ritchie, explains that there "is no one [neural] center for emotion, just as there is none for playing tennis—nor for anything complicated. It involves interactions across different brain areas." This is especially true with respect to fright. The brain employs complex interactive processes to translate sensory data into intelligible, alarming images that, in turn, spark an almost instantaneous response.

Take my near accident. In what seemed like a nanosecond, the back of a gigantic semitrailer suddenly filled my windshield. The first thing my brain did was to take in the image of the menacing semi, initially nothing more than a pattern of light and colors. This image traveled from the retina in my eye (where it was translated into the basic electrical pulse language of the brain), through the optical nerve, to the thalamus. The thalamus is located toward the front of the brain in two sections, one in each hemisphere. Neuroscientists describe the thalamus as a final pit stop for most sensory information in the brain; it is a major fork in the road for data generated by our senses. Most of this data is sent to the visual cortex, where sights and imagery are processed. A smaller portion heads directly to the amgydala and its partner, the hippocampus, to be screened for telltale signs of danger.

When responding to danger, the hippocampus and amygdala act in tandem. The hippocampus is the brain's memory bank. It takes information, such as that generated by the semi, and runs a match program, sifting through its repository of stored images for semis, near collisions, and the like, in search of reasonable facsimiles from past experience to guide the brain's response. The amygdala, an almond-shaped organ located near the center of the brain (*amygdala* is the Greek word for "almond"), adds its input by generating an emotional profile in accordance with the sensory data. Different parts of the amygdala receive different kinds of sensory information. A wonderfully made piece of machinery, it has specialized receptors for each of our senses. The amygdala works like a sorting machine also, matching feelings with images, continually monitoring all sensory information, checking and double-checking our every experience to make sure it has been assigned the right fear factor and therefore generates the appropriate emotional response.

In my encounter with the semi, the amygdala read "Danger!" and reacted immediately. In an ingenious stroke of engineering, it is outfitted with transmitters that reach out to different areas of the brain, each controlling one or more of fear's various symptomatic responses. For instance, it reports to the brain's system for gross motor movement, which slammed my foot on the brakes. Simultaneously, it sent instructions to the center that controls my facial muscles, which in turn pulled my mouth into the telltale oval of fright and tightened my vocal cords for a scream. Upon recognizing danger, the amygdala overrides all other mental systems and functions, orchestrating the body's complete energy and attention to mastermind an escape. It is both the lookout and commanding officer of the fear SWAT team.

In addition to responding to multiple alarm dangers, the brain works more subtly through the voice of intuition. Here, onto the screen of our mind, fear sentries post the occasional pop-up warning that we should be on guard, having perhaps entered unwittingly into what very well could be actual danger.

A woman walks down a sidewalk toward the front door of her apartment building just after dusk. As she reaches into her pocketbook and rustles about for the keys—*ping*—a slight shiver runs down her spine. A tiny, flashing warning light blinks on. "That shadow lurking in the entryway is a mugger." She knows it probably isn't, but prudence and experience combine to heighten her vigilance. Instead of walking directly in, she loops past her door and looks back from a better angle, either to see the coatrack that is casting the ominous shadow or the stranger whose presence her intuition sensed. Though intuition may misdirect us, we shouldn't dismiss it out of hand. Many report having been rescued from real danger by premonition, a kind of sixth sense or fear-focused ESP. Most of us have at least one story about a premonition that kept us from harm's way.

Whether it arrests our attention bluntly through a full-body alert or more subtly through intuition, fright functions like the pain reflex wired to our sense of touch. People born without a sense of touch feel no pain, at least no physical pain. But whatever advantage freedom from pain might seem to offer is overwhelmed by its attendant dangers. With touch on the blink, the other four senses must work over-time to make sure that their host human is not resting his hand on a live burner.

Should we ever regret how jumpy we sometimes are (af-ter a shoulder tap, say, or encounter with a coatrack), we need only remember this: the very few people whose amyg-dalas are compromised for some reason and therefore don't function correctly do not experience fright. Dangerous situ-ations do not come to their attention the way they do the rest of us. For example, since their brains are not hardwired for a fear of falling, such people cannot walk safely along the top of a cliff. In such an instance, fright is liberating. Call it "freedom through fear." We can climb cliffs safely— and do hundreds of other things—only because our fear centers tell us when to be afraid.

WORRY

Worry, our second fear, springs from an active (often overactive) imagination. A little knowledge can be a terrifying thing.

It's easy to see why this fear in particular—mixing a little knowledge with an active imagination—provides such perfect fodder for the Internet. Distributing fear factoids to a susceptible public, new Web sites mushroom daily on everything from earthquakes to bed lice. (No one, it turns out, sleeps alone.) One such site pokes fun at worry itself. Dedicating its pages to "questioning the wisdom of FDR's statement daily," fear.com suggests that *many* things are more frightening than fear itself.

Here is how fear.com works. Participants submit their favorite worries, and an interactive audience votes on whether it shares these fears. Submitted fears run the gamut from smallpox to monkeypox, from global warming to one person's fear that our planet is getting colder (hundreds agree). Judging from the number of votes cast—more often pro than con—fear.com has touched a nerve. Among the more popular fears:

- Anyone can terrorize the country if he's smart enough.

- Someone is watching you all the time.

- Abundant electromagnetic radiation is slowly killing you.

- Pretty soon everything will in some way cause cancer.

To the extent that visitors to fear.com end up laughing at their own silliness, the site has value. But entertaining fears is dangerous. Reading that certain people are scared to stand in front of a working microwave plants a worry seed somewhere in our brain, even though the fear is groundless. The next time we stand in front of a microwave, some overzealous sentinel in our consciousness—a mercenary from somebody else's army—will blast his tinny little trumpet in alarm. "That's ridiculous," we say to ourselves. But part of us wonders. It wants us to step back. It wants to protect us from getting zapped.

The most troubling fear I found among the hundreds listed on fear.com is "that fear.com is a metaphor for life." Though obviously tongue-in-cheek, this cautionary note contains just enough truth to be unsettling. Judging from the thousands of deadly serious sites dedicated to fears such as the ones people confess to there, anyone who may be worried that "the Internet will be the next target of terrorism" is way behind the times. Every form of media feeds the fear frenzy; all it takes is a new microbe and a decent graphic artist. But the Internet abets terror in a targeted way. We select the one thing that worries us most, do a global search, and gain instant access to hundreds of virtual petri dishes in which to culture our fear.

I certainly don't mean to make light of real terrorism. But

here, too, fear itself can be more scary than its source. We fulfill every terrorist's fondest dream when we compound the terror he might actually inflict by placing into his hands the weapon of our own imagination. Describing the impact of terrorism on the nation's psyche, one business writer underscored fear's cost by rescripting a well-known television commercial. "Duct tape: $7.50; plastic sheeting: $17.95; damage to the American economy: incalculable." People who now own a lifetime supply of duct tape have succeeded in terrorizing themselves more than they have in protecting themselves from terror.

My own fear of terrorism peaks when I am standing in line at the airport to pass through security. As I fret over whether I am going to make my plane, pictures of guns, bombs, and poison with a red slash cutting through them turn my worry toward the possibility my plane will be hijacked. "Of course it won't," I say to myself intelligently and firmly, but the presence of armed guards continues to instruct my mind to gird for danger. Though the government beefed up airport security precisely to ensure that terrorists will have a harder time hijacking planes than ever before, rather than diminishing, my worry grows in response to this security. Worry's logic can be described generously as "often irrational." Once temporarily trapped inside security itself, I can't help but wonder whether a real criminal is beating the system while the rest of us are unbuckling our pants and waiting for our shoes.

Worry wreaks havoc on more than just our nerves. Untempered, it can lead to full-blown phobia, whereby the fear reflex is dragooned into the service of an inner obsession, triggering the same response that an overpowering outer stimulus does with sudden fright.

Worry can also undermine our health and mental equilibrium more subtly. Scientific studies document how worry eats away at the body while gnawing at the mind—literally. Recent findings suggest that prolonged worry and anxiety may lead to memory loss and brain damage. Dr. Robert Sapolsky of Stanford University discovered that when the body experiences chronic fear-related stress, the adrenal gland secretes steroid hormones called glucocorticoids. Over a lifetime, these hormones collect near the hippocampus, the region of the brain that stores memory and collaborates with the amygdala in outwitting danger. If after many years the hormones reach a certain level, they create a toxic atmosphere, impairing our capacity to recall memories and to perform basic tasks.

Admittedly, such research, together with other fear-related studies, does give us at least one perfectly good reason to worry: worry is a killer. In addition to chipping away at our memory, it can raise blood pressure and add to our stress level, shortening life expectancy. Since a foreshortened life is among the things we worry about most, enlightened self-interest suggests that less worry could well serve our long-term goals better than enhanced vigilance.

Safety is overrated to begin with. Gavin de Becker (one of the fear experts featured in my *Freedom from Fear* Book Club) defines the word *safe* as "free of acceptable risk." In other words, anyone who is dead runs no risk of being killed. As if this were not ironic enough, we can be perfectly safe and still be gripped by fear. We must never underestimate just how successful an alarmist worry can be. Slap a shark on the cover of *People* magazine and even folks who live in Nebraska will snatch it up to cringe at the danger (as we all have since the movie *Jaws* came out thirty years ago).

Sharks make great fear copy. Merciless, beady, dagger eyes; multiple rows of sharp, crooked, serrated teeth; capped by the specter of a single fin cutting through the water, death's instrument itself gliding stealthily beneath the surface, a torpedo-like dark shadow homing in on its next helpless target—which *could* be us! We don't experience shark panics every summer; to keep fresh, fear alternates its copy. But every decade or so, with no greater rationale than could have been marshaled the summer before, sharks capture the headlines during August's dog days. How dangerous are sharks? Not very, in the scale of things. The odds are thirty times greater that one will be struck by lightning than killed by a shark. Millions fewer people are killed every year by sharks than by malaria-infected mosquitoes—the actual ratio is several hundred thousand to one. If you choose not to swim in the ocean, the likelihood that you will be attacked by a shark slips from almost nil (greater odds than against your winning millions in the lottery) to zero (the odds you have of winning if you don't buy a ticket).

During the summer of 2001, right before 9/11, America went through one of its periodic shark obsessions. Five shark fatalities were recorded in 2001, down from twelve the year before. Yet by late August, the nation was all in a dither. *Time* magazine devoted its cover to this terror, giving rise to the moniker "Summer of the Shark." Though immediately forgotten in the wake of real drama two weeks later, television specials and newspaper reports from the front lines of Miami all the way to Omaha chronicled the unfolding drama for an apparently transfixed public. *USA Today* assembled an unintentionally hilarious list of helpful tips, "What you should do repelling an attacking shark." First item on the list: "Don't try to pry open its jaws. More than likely, you will get bitten."

How pathetic and self-indulgent it feels now to have wasted any emotional energy whatsoever on the danger posed by sharks the week before true terror struck. But fear always finds an object. Lacking something worth worrying about, the human imagination fixes on anything, however miniscule the danger. With more credible targets, fear still exaggerates, just more persuasively. For this reason, the Summer of the Shark remains a blinking red light, at which we should pause whenever we begin to get terrified, even by things that present demonstrated danger. When the mind encounters a monster worthy of its imagination, it cannot resist applying its full artistic scope to that monster's magnification. Fear equips us with 3-D glasses and projects manufactured horror onto a huge screen.

Worry grows in direct proportion to how little influence we have, or feel we have, over what may happen in the future. The less we can do to change things, the more terrified we are of them. Maybe we prefer monsters, however distant, whose menace lies beyond our control, because such monsters allow us the luxury of victimhood. When there is nothing to do but cower, we are off the hook.

That we worry more about things we can't change than about dangers we can take action to avoid underscores the perversity of worry's logic. The same person who cancels a vacation because she is worried that somebody might hijack her plane may smoke cigarettes, drink too heavily, or drive without her seat belt fastened and not think twice about it. The mortal odds posed by her own actions (statistics she somehow manages to ignore) are exponentially greater than those posed by the thing she fears. Not only that, but she could lower them on command. If she buckled up, stopped smoking, or restricted herself to a drink a day, she—not to mention her fellow passengers through life—would be markedly less in jeopardy. Forget for a moment about the morality involved in such decisions. Think of it as enlightened self-interest. If she did these things, rationally speaking, she would have less to fear. The word *worry* stems from the Anglo-Saxon root meaning "strangle" or "choke." How can we break worry's stranglehold and keep it from choking us? By loosening our own grip on the other end of its noose.

Another reason that sharks (and terrorists, for that matter) worry our minds so much is that we have a higher tolerance for familiar risks than for fresh or exotic ones. Acquaintance always leaves us less vulnerable to hearsay. Therefore, even once-exotic illnesses such as the West Nile virus or Lyme disease had a relatively short fear shelf life (as, almost certainly, will SARS and bird flu). By its fourth summer, people were still dying of the West Nile virus, and Lyme disease continues to elude simple detection and a dependable cure. But discounting these now more familiar dangers as increasingly marginal, we are beginning to pay the threat they pose to our safety less (and therefore more appropriate) mind. We can still afford to shift more of our summer fear quotient from exotic terrors that claim relatively few victims to the demonstrably more democratically lethal effects of ultraviolet radiation from the sun. Here, rather than worry, all we need do is slap on some sunscreen and put on a hat.

Familiarity raises our tolerance for things that can prove dangerous (cars, say, or jaywalking) because we build up trust in things we experience as being acceptably risky. I probably shouldn't jaywalk, but jaywalking is one of the things people in New York City do. I would estimate having jaywalked about 25,000 times in my life. Yet that I have never been hit by a car is, statistically, not the least bit remarkable. The odds of my getting killed jaywalking are miniscule. But not as miniscule as the odds of my being killed by a terrorist. Even if the incidence of terrorism in the United States should quadruple from its average over the past ten years (including 9/11), our risk of dying from anthrax, smallpox, suicide bombings, and hijackings combined will remain far lower than the odds of our being killed by a car while walking across the street.

Given how dangerous life is, we may profitably take time

out from our shark, terrorist, and SARS worries to pay at
least glancing attention to the fact that somehow none of
the millions of dangerous things that lurk in life's shadows
waiting to terminate our lives has actually yet managed to
do so. One day this will happen, whether we worry about it
in advance or not. Trapdoors do finally swing open and
roofs cave in. In the meantime, however, the most frequent
injuries we suffer are psychological. Worrying about what
may finally kill us is to die a thousand deaths before our appointed time.

People do get killed jaywalking. And they get killed by terrorists, Lyme disease, West Nile virus, SARS, and bird flu.
Weighed on the scale of life's dangers, however, on average
each poses what we may dare call an acceptable risk, and
not to accept acceptable risks is irrational. More rational by
far is to weigh the danger in any given situation proportion-
ally. Should fear slip in a hand to tip the scales, slap it away.

One final word about worry. Marcel Proust observed that
"only that which is absent can be imagined." Whenever we
worry about something that might happen to us, we can
be assured of only one thing: it is absent. The very thing we
are fretting over poses no present danger, for it does not yet
exist. You won't find this message included on fear.com or in
any of fear's compelling media-sponsored advertisements.
The reason is simple. Once you figure it out, you'll be that
much more reluctant to purchase a time-share from one of
worry's salesmen and vacation with imaginary sharks.

GUILT

Our third fear is guilt. Guilt and fear may strike you as being different things, but the two are intrinsically related. Whenever guilt takes possession of the conscience, it arrives hand in hand with fear—the fear of getting caught. Bad behavior may prompt this fear. Or perfectionism. Guilt runs the spectrum from useful to pointless. But whatever its cause, guilt always keeps company with shame and secrets. Secrecy, in turn, abets guilt by excluding us from the circle of forgiveness, where guilt is absolved.

A full quarter of my counseling sessions revolve around guilt. If it takes a person twenty minutes before he can confess what he's come in to speak to me about, I can almost count on guilt being the culprit. He may have a perfectly good reason to feel guilty, but often his mind has turned a misdemeanor into a felony. "You will be shocked when I tell you this," he says, hoping perhaps to soften the coming blow. When I assure him—after drawing out the particulars of his story—that I am not the least bit shocked, I often sense that he thinks I am being kind, not truthful. This is because guilt condemns and sentences us without a fair trial. When we finally work up the courage to present our case to a jury of our peers—which, in a way, is what we are doing when we go to a counselor—we may be amazed at how quickly (and justifiably) we win forgiveness. Until that moment comes, however, guilt's shadow is so long that we must live in darkness to keep it hidden.

Secrets and lies go together. One way guilt strengthens its grip is by begging us to lie to protect our secrets, thereby isolating and estranging us from the very people who could help absolve our guilt by forgiving us (if we are appropriately contrite). It also makes us guiltier and, therefore, more fearful. In addition to the crime, we now have to worry about the cover-up. Once we turn ourselves in, however, no one can capture us—the fear of being caught is over.

This explains why guilt thrives only in darkness. When tested in the light of day, the shadows that haunt us may disappear. Even when they don't—when we have done something bad for which we should be ashamed or punished—nine times out of ten the best way to neutralize guilt is to own up to it. Whenever the simple truth proves less destructive than a web of lies (that is to say, almost always), trusting the truth is better than cowering from it. Should our honesty have consequences, fear is still diminished. No punishment is harder on a guilty conscience than getting away scot-free.

Among those who knew how powerful secrets can be were the ancient Gnostics. These Jewish and Christian sects in the centuries immediately preceding and following the life of Jesus placed their faith in knowledge (hence their name, from *gnosis*, the Greek word for "knowledge"). Soon going the way of most religious splinter groups, they broke into smaller and smaller pieces until they disappeared from history. But one of their insights abides. The Gnostics' secret to getting into heaven can help us address fear on earth.

One sect of Gnostics held that there are seven heavens, each more glorious than the last, whose gates are guarded by supernatural bouncers called archons. These archons are forbidding characters, determined to keep mere mortals from entering the celestial realm. You can't fight them. And you can't fool them. The only way to crack the code of an otherwise divine security system is to look each archon directly in the eye and call him by his true name. The Gnostics realized that to name something correctly is to possess power over it. So they taught one another the archons' names.

Though the Gnostics were seeking knowledge of heaven's secrets, their insight holds true for earthly knowledge as well. Naming is power. By naming our fears, we can break their control over our lives. The process is one of discovery, not only to "know thyself" but also, in the argot of the theater, to "reveal thyself." The very things we are most hesitant to reveal, both to ourselves and to others, lie at the root of our guilt. They also compound it. When we fear getting caught for having done something bad, we become more defensive. Accused of the tiniest infraction, we leap to justify ourselves. It is as if we have a magnet in our brain that guilt makes stronger. The only way to weaken this magnet is to remove its power source, by naming and eliminating causes for shame.

A man I was counseling introduced me to the guilt magnet. Though I had observed this phenomenon for years, his comments suggested a possible name for it. "It's like I have this thing in my head that attracts criticism," he said. "All a cop has to do is look at me sideways and I jump to attention and feel like turning myself in."

By "cop," I soon discovered, what he really meant was "wife." He told me how he would enter his apartment in the evening, seemingly fine after an acceptably productive day, only to find himself off-balance the moment she would challenge him about something he had forgotten to do. The presenting cause of their ensuing argument rarely mattered. What mattered was how quickly (and to what devastating effect) her accusation, even her tone of voice, would activate his guilt magnet.

I remember the precise illustration he offered to describe how this worked, because it was so magnificently ordinary. One evening he forgot to pick up the milk his wife had asked him to get on his way home from work. This is when one is supposed to say, "I'm sorry," and change the subject (or better yet, go out and get the milk). But he couldn't leave it there. Opting for capital punishment instead, he somehow found a way to escalate the milk issue into a wholly unnecessary confrontation pivoting on his fundamental worthlessness.

"What's going on?" she asked. "You are overreacting."

"I am *not* overreacting," he insisted.

"No, something is wrong. What's really the matter?"

"*Nothing* is the matter," he snapped.

He told me that at first, when trapped in such a predicament, he honestly couldn't explain what was going on or what really was the matter, because he didn't know the answer himself. Unable to account for his defensiveness, all he could do was let his guilt take over. Accuse him of forgetting to bring home milk and, if the emotional planets were misaligned, his guilt magnet would attract every shard of shame sequestered in his conscience and leave him feeling like a worm. Almost invariably, his overpowering sense of shame would provoke an unnecessary secondary quarrel for which he knew himself to be almost wholly responsible.

This man had come into my study not to talk about problems he was having with his wife but about the problem he was having with alcohol. For years he had poured alcohol down his escape hatch. He recognized that until he stopped drinking, he could do little about the destabilizing fear secretly eating away at his soul. Having named alcohol as the source of his fear, he was now in a position to neutralize its power.

I didn't tell him what to do, though I shared a success story or two that might give him courage. Even if I had offered him a set of instructions, my words would have held little authority. Even as contrition precedes our right to forgiveness, to free ourselves from guilt we have to spring the lock ourselves, for its door opens only from the inside. By the time he called on me, he knew this. It had finally dawned on him that the reason he was so easily thrown, even by the smallest accusation, was he felt so guilty about his drinking. After years of bargaining, half measures, and procrastination—favored techniques for holding fear's rapt attention—he at last had the good sense to choose self-respect (and his life) over the bottle. That very week he joined Alcoholics Anonymous, made plans to enter a rehabilitation clinic, and thereby set forth on the road toward recovery.

To free ourselves from fear, we often have to walk through it. This man had to confess to his wife what she already knew despite his recurring angry denials—she was right, he was powerless over alcohol. He then had to request a month-long leave from work to enter rehab, which meant revealing his secret to a boss who previously had known only that her coworker had become increasingly defensive and undependable of late. To his surprise, his boss then revealed that she was about to fire him. Now, if rehabilition worked, the man could have a second chance with his job. But it was when he worked up the courage to confess to his friends that the strangest thing happened. They congratulated him! They told him how much they admired his courage. One of them even asked for help; he, too, might have a problem with alcohol, but he had been afraid to talk to anyone about it and hadn't known where to turn. Courage can be contagious, too.

There are two ways to deionize our guilt magnets. The perfectionists among us can do so by lightening up; those of us who are guilty for good reason can change our behavior. This man needed to change before he could lighten up, but both techniques work. Like forgetting to bring home milk, most of our crimes are not even misdemeanors; they are fully included in life's entry fee. Sometimes, however, guilt can be good for us. In this man's case, the guilt that was destroying his relationship with his wife was the thing that finally saved him.

One further result of his decision to quit drinking— unexpected by him but completely predictable—was that his guilt magnet slowly lost its power. Consequently, other aspects of his conscience improved. He told me the story about the milk—now ancient history for him—six months after our first meeting. He was well on his way to recovery and we could laugh together about how gargantuan his guilt had grown, until he named its source and reduced its power. He confessed to me then that he no longer fretted all that much about the many little things he still did wrong. This made perfect sense to me. Having addressed what was in his higher interest to correct, he could now afford to pay less attention to his share of universal human foibles. Without a major sin charging up his guilt magnet, the little sins he committed over the course of any given day no longer disrupted his peace of mind. His conscience wasn't pure by any means, but it was clear.

These days, he told me, when he "forgets the milk" (his term now for any little mistake he may make), his wife still gets mad. The difference is, he doesn't go crazy. Should she accuse him, no doubt justly, of taking his responsibilities to the household too lightly, he tries to take her concerns seriously, and realizes that he should probably take them more seriously than he does. But he doesn't spin out of control when she gets angry with him. And soon the world changes subjects, which it always will if we are patient. He and his wife are then free to drift happily onward into another evening of each other's company.

INSECURITY

Our fourth fear is insecurity. Rather than the fear of getting caught for doing something wrong, insecurity is the fear of getting noticed for *being* somehow wrong—out of place, conspicuous, literally or figuratively "improperly dressed." If worry haunts our minds and guilt calls us to the bar of conscience, insecurity triggers feelings of emotional inadequacy.

When we are asked to rate the things that scare us most, public speaking almost always tops the list. No wonder. It presents insecurity with the perfect opening. We are standing in front of a group of people whose eyes are fixed upon us, on the lookout for the slightest flaw in appearance or delivery. Even those of us who speak in public all the time must walk through our fear on the way to the podium. Once we begin, our feelings of inadequacy abate, but let a single person get up and walk out in the middle of what we are saying and these feelings return with a vengeance. If we happen to lose our place or forget our train of thought, fear freezes us. Insecurity turns into panic.

Insecurity can strike at any time, even when we are sleeping. Most so-called anxiety dreams are basically insecurity dreams. One version familiar to many of us is set in school. It is the last week of classes and we are about to graduate. But then we remember that we have one more exam to take. Unfortunately, this test is on a subject that we know nothing about. Our graduation hinges on passing this course. So close to success, we are certain now to fail and can't do a thing about it. I must have had some version of this dream dozens of times when I was in school and over the following years. But since entering the ministry, the same nightmare has mostly taken a vocational turn. It has to do with public speaking.

It is Sunday morning. I have lost track of the time, if not the entire day. Suddenly I realize that I am on in five minutes. I don't have my robe. I don't have my manuscript. In a panic, I rush through the church offices—a suddenly unfamiliar rabbit warren—desperately searching first for my robe and sermon and then for the sanctuary. This search is thwarted by locked doors and labyrinthine passageways. Finally I happen upon the door to the chancel, entering a church full of expectant worshippers.

Off-balance already, at this point in the dream I begin to unravel completely. The service has already begun; my papers are out of order; I can't find my Bible for the reading; when I do, I can't find my place in it; I begin speaking anyway, making things up as I go along; the microphone doesn't work, so no one can hear my voice; people get restive and begin leaving; I rush to plug in the sound system and get tangled in a snake pit of wires; returning to the chancel, I have no idea where we are in the liturgy and can't find my order of worship; I look out and the church is half empty; I happen to glance down, horrified to discover I'm wearing no pants; I begin preaching, without a clue as to what I am saying; only a few worshippers are left in the pews; I decide to offer the benediction but can't remember how it goes, so I run for the exit; and then I wake up.

Lawyers tell me they sometimes dream of showing up in the wrong courtroom or without their briefcase. Doctors find themselves in the middle of a complicated operation unable to place their hands on the necessary surgical instruments. Teachers can't find their classrooms and when they do, the children get up and leave. Perhaps the most harrowing anxiety dream I have ever heard came courtesy of a waitress I was counseling. With her as its hapless star, it included everything that could possibly go wrong in a restaurant.

Despite their distinctive settings, there are elements common to such dreams. Whether we find ourselves in a meeting, outdoors in a crowd, or riding in a packed elevator, most of us have had the sinking experience of looking down to discover that we forgot to put on our pants. That's precisely what insecurity feels like—being naked in public.

To feel exposed is to feel inadequate. We shouldn't beat ourselves up over this. Not everyone suffers from an occasionally fragile ego, but those who don't may have other problems; the old psychological term for individuals who never feel unsure of themselves is "character disorder." Most of us, however, could afford a little less insecurity—a little less concern about appearances. We can get so tangled up in our emotional underwear that it is hardly possible to walk into a room without feeling vulnerable. Cringing from the imagined judgment of others—who are fretting more over their own emotional wedgies than anyone else's—we succumb instead to the merciless critic within.

Why do we feel inadequate as often as we do? For one thing, being human is intrinsically awkward. We are not driven only by instinct. We make thousands of little decisions every day, from the moment we wake up in the morning to right before we drift off to sleep at night. The simplest doubt—did we choose the right clothes when we got dressed this morning?—can keep us off-balance all day long. Because we doubt ourselves, we naturally assume that others must be questioning us as well, shaking their heads as we pass, wondering what we could possibly have been thinking when we pulled that particular combination out of the closet. Insecurity is self-consciousness. Rather than being conscious *of* the world around us, we fixate on how we appear *to* the world around us.

With the possible exception of worry, insecurity is the most contagious of fears. We catch it from one another in a backhanded way. For instance, one person may compensate for her feelings of insecurity by putting others down. She doesn't become any more secure by so doing, but those whom she puts down certainly feel less secure. As sensitive as she may be to criticism or slights, she is utterly insensitive to how her own words or actions may be hurtful. This drives others away, which adds to her own insecurity by isolating her from the kinds of personal connections that might help her overcome it. Insecurity is rooted in isolation, an isolation we more often create than inherit. Either we drive people away or we run from them.

Insecurity accompanies us into unfamiliar situations. One parishioner laughingly told me that when she walks into a room full of strangers, her hands begin to grow. What is she to do with these conspicuous, throbbing hands? I told her that this is one reason men have pockets in their trousers. Since she wears dresses, I more helpfully suggested that next time she might consider avoiding all eye contact and finding, if possible, a bulletin board or kiosk posted with dozens of notices. Read the notices, I said. Over time, I told her, her hands will probably begin to shrink. Then, with hands the size of everybody else's, she may be ready for the room. I did add that if she's looking for a shortcut, all she has to do is go up to somebody who is standing all alone and introduce herself. Odds are, he will be just as relieved as she to be thinking about someone other than himself. This whole conversation may sound silly to you, but it never feels silly when we are crippled by self-consciousness.

All forms of fear trigger a fight-or-flight response—we either defend ourselves or run for cover. One problem with insecurity is that both fight and flight make it worse. Charles Darwin observed that "the free expression by outward signs of an emotion intensifies it." Even as brooding on our anger makes us angrier, emotional insecurity feeds itself. By "fighting" it, we get more entangled in it. "Fleeing" such feelings doesn't solve the problem, either. When we bury emotions, they fester.

Since insecurity is a form of narcissism, the secret to overcoming it lies in breaking the grip of self-absorption. As with my parishioner's throbbing hands, most insecurity ranges from unnecessary to senseless. Little things that may possibly happen to expose or embarrass us—all the million "mortifying" ways in which we can, figuratively speaking, spill tomato juice down the front of our shirt—won't cause much of a blip on any radar screen except our own. Therefore, when we find ourselves fixating on our inadequacies, the best thing to do is turn off our own monitor and tune in to someone else's. Group therapy is often successful because, by listening to others, we discover that they feel just as inadequate as we do. Problem solving with a friend also places our problems in perspective. The mirrors we look into improve greatly when the thing that catches our attention in them isn't us.

In addition to finding strength in numbers, we may seek it by sneaking a peak at the clock. One member of my congregation has come up with the "one hour rule" about any experience she is emotionally at sea about—chairing a meeting, say, or delivering a speech. In one hour, more or less, it will be over. And what's an hour in the context of an entire life? When we neglect the "one hour rule," insecurity can pervade our entire existence. To counter it, we need only remember, first, that we are not alone, and, second, that the feeling will soon pass.

The ultimate goal is to devote our precious attention to something more abiding than mere appearances. Life's occasions may seem longer when we fret our way through them one painful minute at a time, but time exists to lose ourselves in, not to count.

When we lose ourselves, time passes like a dream, not a nightmare. Then, should someone ask us how people responded to what we wore to life's big party, we won't need to ponder the answer. We came as we were; it's as simple as that. We *can* recall loosening our collar and kicking off our shoes. Our hands? All we really remember is the hand we were holding. What a night it was. The life of the party, we danced until morning. Unafraid of the darkness, we saw in the dawn.

DREAD

Our fifth and final fear is dread, a particularly crippling form of anxiety driven by the desire to control things that lie beyond our control.

Anxiety is the catch-all fear. I don't list it separately, because it employs every trick in fear's book, projecting fright, worry, guilt, and insecurity one by one across the mind's screen. When life feels out of control, all the little things that flash across our mind seem more ominous than they likely are. Often the best way to cope with anxiety is to move from the big picture to the little picture. By breaking anxiety down into its constituent parts, we can get a handle on it, one fear at a time.

Dread (not so much anxiety writ large as anxiety writ dark) is more difficult. It takes our entire future—which really does lie beyond our control—and casts a pall over it. The epitome of negative thinking, dread paints such a bleak picture that any attempt to shine light on the subject seems in vain. When everyday anxiety—which we all experience— takes a fatalistic turn, we project our mishmash of worries, guilt, and insecurity onto the screen of an endless tomorrow.

The specific mental illness most often associated with dread is depression. When we enter the dark world of depression, our defenses become our trap. We cut ourselves off from things that might actually save us. Whatever its trigger, depression takes on a life of its own, in many cases biologically rooted and therefore susceptible to the right medication or otherwise treatable through psychotherapy. Taken more broadly—as a metaphor for dread—it represents the triumph of hopelessness over anything we might do to reduce such feelings. By isolating us, dread cuts us off from the sources that might allay it.

We feel dread when a loved one dies and we decide that we will never experience joy again. We feel it when we have failed in some profound and painful way. The collapse of an important relationship or doing poorly at work can trigger dread (as can failing to achieve a relationship or find work). When anxious, we are at loose ends; with dread we feel discarded. Dread bleeds the color out of our existence.

In its most familiar form, dread combines the fear of death with a fear of life. Aware of life's fragility, yet with a diminished appreciation for its preciousness, we look for stability and predictability where neither can be found. Every risk we might take to splash some color into our lives strikes us as either imprudent or so hopeless that we might as well not take the chance. We say to ourselves, "Nothing ventured, nothing lost."

Dread also expresses itself in a fear that lies at the heart of the human predicament—the fear of abandonment. As long as we live, we are never safe from loss. Others leave us along life's way. And when our own time comes, life itself abandons us; nothing can prevent our fall.

The fear of falling—not in a physical but in an intellectual, emotional, and even spiritual sense—perfectly describes how dread affects the mind's inner ear. In the felt and frightening tension between being and nonbeing, we experience vertigo. We reach a point where we can no longer abide feelings of vulnerability. For this very reason, dread places physical and emotional invulnerability—safety and security—above all other human goods. If we do not climb, we will not fall.

Our parents teach us the same lesson from the time we are toddlers. We are in the playground, happily swinging away—"Not so high!" they yell. In their temporary role of protectors, understandably they try to keep us safe. Worrying about us and instructing us in life's dangers is a parent's job. But when we are warned repeatedly against expressing curiosity or taking even the slightest risk, our parents' efforts leave a lasting impression.

The overprotected child is not all that much safer than the average toddler. Even when maintained with smothering vigilance, the nick and bruise patrol fails in its objective. Where it succeeds is in creating a frightened adult. After thousands of shrill warnings and half as many repetitions of the solemn words "I told you so," to our impressionable minds curiosity and risk themselves become suspect. Once out in the world on our own, a voice within us echoes, "Not so high!" No wonder fear so effortlessly reigns over the average adult mind.

There are many kinds of loss in life, not only death. As children, we experience the first pangs of abandonment the moment it dawns on us that our parents are not an extension of our own being. The first time we fall into something other than our parents' arms has to be something of a shock. Eventually we get used to it. And then, for a time, we seek it. We run from our parents' arms, so as not to be held back from our own adventures. Finally, having long since learned that our parents are not gods, one day we learn from them what it means to be mortal.

When I am counseling a parishioner who is struggling to come to terms with the impending death of a loved one, often we find ourselves contemplating how the very loss that makes us more wary of life's fragility can at the same time make us more appreciative of life's preciousness. Love and grief come packaged together. We can't have the former without risking the latter. In this sense, grief is essentially good. Dread offers precisely the opposite counsel. "Now you know how bad it feels to be hurt. Never place yourself in the same position again."

The most terrible thing about dread is that it invites death to take up permanent residence in our soul. Conscious that any action we might take hangs suspended under the threat of loss or abandonment, we protect ourselves by muting our dreams and curbing our affections. We can't be abandoned if there is no one to abandon us, so we avoid commitments. We can't lose face if we don't show our face, so we hide in the wings. What's the point in going back to pick up the credits we need to earn our college degree? Why even bother starting that novel we've always wanted to write? Why should anything matter more than anything else? No matter what we do, we will die anyway. So we quit life before being fired.

Not just dread, but all fear preaches caution. In fact, if fear had a mantra, it would be "Better safe than sorry." This advice is easy to follow. Playing it safe makes both emotional and physical sense. The question remains, is it that much better to be safe than to risk the possibility of new friendship, say, or a challenging new job—anything that lifts us off familiar ground? Safety and risk only appear to be mutually exclusive. We must be as cautious about safety as we are about risk. Take no other risks and we still run the danger of leading a sorry life. In fact, when it comes to things that really matter, in exchange for the benefits that risk can bring, sometimes it is better to be sorry than safe.

Even if safety should become our primary objective in life, to keep ourselves safe is impossible. People die in beds and in bathtubs. Joggers die. Vegetarians die. So do nonsmokers and teetotalers. Even people with low cholesterol die. Not to mention the millions who die of complications from anxiety itself. To be free of acceptable risk is not life's goal, but its enemy. By inviting nonbeing to the party years before one's death day, fear protects us not from death but from life.

We can't argue with dread, any more than we can argue with depression. And sometimes, when our world is falling apart, dread and depression make good sense. That we should feel crushed by the loss of someone we love is both fine and inescapable. With grief as love's measure, the more we love, the more we risk to lose and therefore stand to fear. This is necessary fear. When a loved one is fighting for his or her life, we can't help but feel fear's anguish; a shadow falls across our very being. "Why?" we ask ourselves again and again, tormenting our minds with the one unanswerable question. "If only I could do something," we say, even as, unbeknownst only to us, we are probably doing several quite splendid, simply not lifesaving, things. At times such as these—which recur throughout the best ordered life—we must fight to keep dread from draining our lives of color. But to eliminate its influence entirely is impossible.

When suffering overwhelms hope, as it sometimes will, life's burden feels too heavy for us to shoulder; it may *in fact* be too heavy to shoulder on our own. We must then turn to others and to God for strength. And for encouragement. Encouraged, we once again take heart. In the face of dread's most persuasive argument, mustering the courage to act, love, and be, we answer fear's no with a saving yes.

COURAGE

THREE KINDS OF COURAGE

Life is frightening. Accomplished performers get stage fright. The most practiced telemarketer feels a pang of fear every time he picks up the phone to make a cold call. When we walk through the corridors of a hospital, fear accompanies us, as it does when we enter the boss's office for a performance review. Watching a mighty storm from the safety of our kitchen, we cringe at the crack of thunder and lightning. If the doorbell rings when we are not expecting company, we can't help but be scared. We are just as apprehensive as we are angry when a teenage child is out past his or her curfew. Ripping open a long-awaited letter that holds either rejection or acceptance, our hand shakes. And any time we chance under death's shadow—waiting for word after a biopsy or answering a three A.M. phone call—fear knots the pit of our stomach.

Since life is frightening, without courage it would be unbearable. Courage rallies our spirits dozens of times daily. But even when we face down our fears—and you would be amazed how often we succeed in doing precisely that—we are still more conscious of our cowardice than of our courage. We feel the fear over which we triumph at the very moment of triumph itself, yet rarely do we actually *feel* courage. We rally to its call, but we don't feel it. What courageous people feel is fear. It is what soldiers feel. And expectant mothers. And awkward teenage boys when they ask a girl out on a date. In fact, it is what all of us feel in a hundred little ways every day of our lives. We feel frightened and demonstrate courage.

I mention this at the outset because it is difficult to help people find courage when they fail to recognize that they already possess it. Our courage may need considerable bolstering, but the challenge we face is not the seemingly impossible one of weaving courage out of whole cloth. It is to add a significant patch or two to the proven courage we already possess.

Courage, too, can be broken down into categories, in this instance organized according to its objective. Every day we muster three basic kinds of courage: the courage to act, the courage to love, and the courage to be.

THE COURAGE TO ACT

The courage to act is the courage to direct, within our power, the scripting and performance of our life story.

Until we act, our story may unfold but it won't develop; accident, not design, will shape it. To choose between a life we help develop and one that merely unfolds should be easy, yet action—the act of creating our lives—does not come easily to us. This is because most of the ways in which we can win our lives back from fear are themselves scary. We may fail—or succeed, setting us up for greater failure by raising the bar over which we can trip. In fact, we shall never succeed without risking failure, since all success is built on the failures that preceded it.

Disregarding this truth, fear champions security above all else. This stifles our development, because it is impossible to be open to the creative spirit and absolutely secure at one and the same time. At best, we fulfill our roles as other actors' seconds, waiting in life's wings. Nonetheless, the promise of security is seductive. It makes us feel safe.

After trumpeting the advantages of security, fear marshals other reasons against our taking action. What if we look foolish in the process? Or fall under somebody's censure? Besides, things aren't really all that bad. By trying to improve them, what if we actually make our lives worse? These are some of fear's favorite arguments. Enticed by their persuasiveness, how quickly we decide to make things "easy" on ourselves. Cutting corners at fear's direction, we avoid taking actions to free our lives from guilt or reduce our worries by tackling them at their source. Knowing our own and the world's troubles so well, we resign ourselves to them. Finally, to spare ourselves its pain, we discount life's meaning. In short, we yield to the duel temptation of sophisticated resignation and cynical chic.

Finding the courage to act means refusing to succumb to fear's life-denying logic. Should we take action, our life will not become a fairy tale—happily ever after—but it will hold out the promise of a finer, fuller performance. When we remove its script from fear's hands, the story of our life will be something we are eager to develop, not something we are apprehensive to watch unfold.

THE COURAGE TO LOVE

The old adage holds true: when we die, we can't take anything with us. But the poets are right as well: love is immortal. After we depart this earth, the love we have given away lives on in our loved ones' hearts. Imagine looking back over our lives as they are ending—breaking them into a million pieces and asking ourselves what of any real value might endure—the pieces that remain will all carry love's signature.

Why then does it take courage to love? For one thing, because the people we love may die before we do. Dare to love and we instantly become vulnerable, a word that means "susceptible to being wounded." Our mother struggles for life in a hospital, or our son risks his in a distant land. At such moments the courage to love is nothing less than the courage to lose everything we hold most dear. Love another with all our heart and we place our heart in jeopardy, one so great that the world as we know it can disappear between the time we pick up the telephone and when we put it down again. Love is grief's advance party.

Love makes us vulnerable in a second way. Put our heart into the hands of another (lover or hero) and he or she may break it. Or give our heart to a cause. Or to the company for which we work. Every time we give our heart away, we risk having it dashed to pieces. Fear promises a safer path: refuse to give away your heart and it will never be broken. And it's true—armored hearts are invulnerable. We can eliminate a world of trouble from our lives simply by closing our hearts. Yet the trouble from which we are liberating ourselves is necessary trouble. We need it as we need breath. Since the most precious and enduring life work is signed by love, to avoid the risk of love is to cower from life's only perfect promise.

THE COURAGE TO BE

Whether we follow the guidance of faith, the teachings of science, or both, we are destined to spend much of our lives living with unanswered and unanswerable questions. Why did our seven-year-old niece get cancer and die? Why was our next-door neighbors' son born autistic? How could that teenager have killed twelve of his classmates? Are we safe pumping gas, or will some madman shoot at us? Are we going to destroy one another and ourselves in a nuclear Armageddon? Such questions riddle our lives, demanding the courage to be—to be uncertain, to be vulnerable, to be sentenced to life and sentenced to death.

Intrinsic to the courage to be are self-acceptance and forgiveness (given that our loved ones and enemies are no less human than we are). In addition, we must develop a high tolerance for uncertainty. Doing so takes courage because whenever we enter the passage from certainty to uncertainty, fear accompanies us. So many things in life are outside our control. The courage to be embraces the uncertainty that lies hidden between the present moment and our last, which looms beyond our reckoning, as do the fates of those we love. In fact, the only thing over which we have any real power is that tiny but not insignificant part of our shared history that we fix by the actions we take and the way we choose to live.

We can find the courage to be in faith. And in the immortality of love. And in selfless acts that fill our cup as we empty it. In fact, every time we say yes to life in answer to fear's no, we manifest the courage to be. This courage can be as simple as accepting an invitation to a party where we don't know a living soul or as complicated as giving thanks for the life of a dying friend. Where we do not and cannot find the courage to be is in our own personal power. Any rug we lay down can be pulled out from under us. The courage to be is therefore also the courage to *let* be. It is the courage to let go—for dear life—of all we cannot keep, including, finally, life itself.

THE COURAGE TO ACT

We all experience stage fright. The courage to act cuts through it, inspiring us to play our part both boldly and well.

Our lives are dramatic—we perform them. To determine whether the role we are playing has the richness and depth it should, we need to view it with a critic's cold eye. Does the plot of our life hold together, or is it merely episodic, with us wandering in and out of other people's scenes? Is our story going anywhere? Does it make any sense? Is it growing in significance from one act to the next, or is its pulse instead either jumpy or flat? Finally, when it is done, will it have been worth the price of admission—ours or anybody else's? In short, are we living in such a way that our lives will prove worth dying for?

We may be booked from dawn to midnight, balancing twenty plates on a stick, and still, for all that activity, be led around by the nose. Conversely, we may free ourselves from all responsibilities, watching (or ignoring) the sand as it runs through our glass. In either case, we are living reactive, not active, lives—our lives leading us, not we them. Reactive lives run

the gamut from frantic to empty. Active lives are more likely to
be centered and therefore marked by inner calm. Being fully
engaged, a monk can be said to lead an active life. Any single
one of us can, as long as we fill the present with our deeds. Unlike reactive existence, the active life leaves little room on its
agenda for fear.

One way to judge whether our lives are active or reactive—
whether we are leading them or they us—is by how often they
follow an independent script. Fear goes with the grain, chart-
ing out a path of least resistance. Fear wants to spare us trouble. "Why not put it off until tomorrow?" it seductively
suggests. One of fear's secrets is that postponed troubles multiply. Waiting for things to happen rather than making them
happen not only commits us to a reactive posture but leaves
us scrambling for ever more cover. Passive people follow
fear's script. Active people make better role models. They exercise freedom.

Raoul Wallenberg, a young Swedish businessman from a
wealthy family, had reached an impasse in his life. The Wal-
lenbergs are to Sweden what the Rockefellers are to the
United States or the Rothschilds to France. He had anything
he wanted, yet his life lacked a sense of purpose. It was
1943, with the world at war and Sweden a neutral country,
so Wallenberg's life was playing itself out in the wings, far
from the main theater of action. He had passions and convictions, but no stage on which to enact them. His family
dealt with Axis and Allies both, which guaranteed financial
success but placed a burden on his conscience.

Wallenberg's personal transformation is captured in a
story, perhaps apocryphal but certainly true to the spirit of
how he turned his life around. Raoul went to the movie *Pimpernel Smith*, a remake of *The Scarlet Pimpernel*, the story of

a well-born British spy who saves members of the French aristocracy from the guillotine during the Revolution. *Pimpernel Smith* recasts this story into one of French resistance fighters being saved from the Gestapo. The star, Leslie Howard, bore an eerie resemblance to Wallenberg, but it was the story itself (in which a single man, working undercover, saves the day) that may have changed his life. As the story goes, from the moment he walked out of the cinema until his death, Wallenberg—himself one-sixteenth Jewish and proud of his heritage—was on a mission. Given the chance, he determined to rescue as many Jews as possible from extermination.

His journey took him from the training fields of the Swedish army (he enlisted in early 1944) to center stage in the horrors unfolding in Eastern Europe, on special assignment as secretary of the Swedish legation in Budapest. In this position, by giving the Jews in Budapest Swedish passports and maintaining strict vigilance against German attempts to deport to the camps those under his diplomatic charge, Wallenberg saved, by some accounts, 100,000 lives.

When Wallenberg arrived in Budapest in June 1944, Hungary had become the final target of Adolf Hitler's twisted imagination; within three months of the Wehrmacht's occupation of Hungary the previous March, twelve thousand Jews a day were being forced into trains and freighted toward almost certain death. Wallenberg's interference dramatically slowed the exodus from Budapest, frustrating the designs of Adolf Eichmann, Hitler's grand master of "fear itself."

Eichmann knew the war was over, but that didn't stop him from turning yet another country into his personal killing field. One evening Wallenberg arranged to have dinner with him. The confrontation of these two men was as extraordinary as it was tense.

"Look, the war is over. Why don't you call off your people? Why not leave now, while you still can?" Wallenberg asked, adding, in conclusion, "Your genocide plans were doomed from the start."

Eichmann responded, "Don't think that just because you are a diplomat, you are immune from danger." But he knew the war was over, admitting, "When the Russians come, I know they'll shoot me. I'm ready."

Eichmann would eventually suffer the death penalty, but it was Wallenberg whom the Russians shot. Arrested by the Soviets when the Russian army liberated Budapest in 1945, he disappeared into captivity, only to have his death confirmed decades later. Yet before his capture, over a matter of a few brief months, a story that once lacked a guiding theme or purpose had burst forth in full action. Stealing a series of unforgettable scenes, Raoul Wallenberg demonstrated remarkable courage. His biographers have pondered what finally motivated him to turn his life (and thereby so many others' lives) around. Perhaps he did go to the movies one day and saw himself as the protagonist of a more important story than the one he was living. More likely, he recast himself in a larger role by his own reinvention. In either case, throwing away his script, he forged a dynamic character, wrote himself into the human drama with redemptive flourish, and thereby changed the ending of a hundred thousand lives.

When we ponder the magnificent accomplishments of people such as Raoul Wallenberg, it is hard to picture ourselves playing their part. Few of us can say, "Starting today, I am going to set out and begin saving lives." But take the story of almost any hero and break his or her actions into their constituent parts, and instructions for the courage to act will be present in each. If the hero of our own life story simply did the same thing one act at a time, the plot of our life, too, could develop in ways that may seem almost unimaginable to us.

Consider Rudolph Giuliani's performance as mayor of New York City during and after the terrorist attack. Did Mayor Giuliani do anything on 9/11 or in the ensuing weeks that any one of us could not imitate?

The answer is no. Giuliani's leadership offers a template for action that everyone can use. His response to crisis was solution- not problem-driven, as good a recipe for staring fear down as any I know. The same solution-driven approach contributed to his successful management of what almost everyone before had called an unmanageable city. It was essential following 9/11.

First, Giuliani didn't panic. The city's Emergency Control Center was right next to the Twin Towers, and he barely escaped being trapped underground, making decisions on the run as he and his advisers encountered one blocked exit after another. Adding another source of anxiety, Washington was under attack as well as New York. When the mayor was connected not with the president but with the vice president and then the phone went dead, he surely could not help but wonder, first, whether the president himself had been harmed and, second, if the White House had now been hit as well as the Pentagon. "I realized that we were in a lot of danger," he said later. "But at the time, there really wasn't time to think about it." Mayor Giuliani was so fully present to the demands of the moment that worry couldn't paralyze him.

During the first hours, the mayor did a number of things that reduced the specter of fear surrounding the city. He called on psychiatrists to advise him on how best to convey breaking news to a shocked citizenry. He knew that little more than solace could be offered to the families of those who had been trapped in the Twin Towers. Having by then learned from the city's medical examiner, Dr. Charles S.

Hirsch, that "most of the bodies would be vaporized," his response, when asked about the fatality count during the first press conference, was compassionate yet unadorned. "When we get the final number, it will be more than we can bear," the mayor said. From the outset of the tragedy, Giuliani never once promised to do more than he could, however little that might seem.

Yet somehow he managed to hearten an entire city. What the terrorists were "trying to do, which is to instill fear in us," would fail, he declared. "Nothing that is borne out of fear and terror can stand in the way of courage, strength, and faith." One by one, the shaken citizens of New York City began to believe this. When he took his daughter, Caroline, to Ground Zero, Rudy added, "It's my job to do for my kids what my father did for me—try to help them figure out how to deal with fear. How to live life, even though you are afraid." He insisted that we view this crisis as an opportunity. Leaving the question "Why?" aside, Giuliani told us, "The thing we have to focus on now is getting the city through this and surviving and being stronger for it."

Every element of the courage to act is present here. To focus on solutions, not problems. To do what we can, no more but also no less. To remember that courage operates in fear's company, but not at its direction. To recognize the opportunity disguised by danger at a time of crisis and to seize it. To stay focused in the present. To ask ourselves not "Why?" but "Where do I go from here?"

To the question "Where do I go from here?" whatever answer we come up with must always include the word *together*. None of us acts alone. We are all part of a larger company. The courage to act leads us to participate in a larger sympathy. If our story speaks to everyone's condition, not just to our own, it may not make great theater, but whatever twists the plot may take, when the curtain falls our play will end well.

To the question "When?"—as in "When should I begin to turn my life around?"—the answer is always "now." We can ponder acting in the future, but the best intentions, however admirable, merely point out that we haven't yet made good on them. We act only in the present.

In a movie or play, the present is intensified. We lose ourselves in the action. According to one handbook on drama, the actor's ultimate goal is "to make seamless the relation between past and present, intention and act, character and actor, mind and body, script and performance." In our own lives as well, the key to fulfilling and enhancing our potential is to become fully present. As we become "present" to others, others become more "present" to us. *Present* here means three things: (1) being accounted for, (2) inhabiting the moment, and (3) offering ourselves as a gift. We can only reconcile ourselves to the past and change the future in the present tense.

When Raoul Wallenberg and Rudy Giuliani were thrust onto history's stage, they performed parts larger than the ones for which they had been cast. Fear created a vacuum and they filled it. By so doing, they became "role models." To find courage, we all seek role models. Then our performance, too, becomes a model to emulate—for our children, friends, coworkers, and neighbors. Even if Wallenberg's *Pimpernel Smith* inspiration is apocryphal, the story reflects how courage works. One great performance inspires another. Leslie Howard inspired Raoul Wallenberg, who has since been played by Richard Chamberlain. James Woods portrayed Rudolph Giuliani, and we can only imagine the effect on some young girl who viewed the docudrama (easier for her to follow than the news itself had been) and decided to commit herself to a life of public service.

At our finest, we are all actors. The well-lived life springs from the well-played role. We are also part of a company. We learn the art of acting from others. They model the courage to act, teaching us how to overcome stage fright and hit the mark. Yet the courage to act is by itself not enough. Even as no one truly acts alone, we need one another's inspiration for a second, in ways more elusive, courage—the courage to love.

THE COURAGE TO LOVE

Fear, not hate, is the opposite of love. We can actually love and hate the same person at the same time; people close to us matter that much. Fear and love cannot coexist, however. They exclude each other. By the same token, desire and love work at cross purposes. Desire is fear-charged longing. It draws on a well of emptiness—measuring what we want by what we lack. Neither can love coexist with violence, whether physical or emotional. What may seem like love is instead love's most pathetic look-alike: masochism. Codependent love is fear-driven also, as is any love that expresses itself through mutual entanglement rather than mutual liberation.

True love is complete the moment we express it. Its gift and receipt are simultaneous. We may think we love another when our love is unrequited and we languish moonstruck and despondent, but what we are actually experiencing— wanting what we lack—is a dream of love. This dream may come true one day and turn into love, but when sponsored by fear, it is more likely to be compromised from the outset by the desire for possession.

We do not and cannot possess the ones we love, for we hold them on loan—a hard truth, making the courage to love also the courage to lose. This dual courage speaks most eloquently when everything we cherish is in jeopardy—when all our expectations for the way life ought to be are interrupted and challenged by death.

I'm just a regular guy," Michael told me the day he died. Perhaps he was worried that I might make too much of his courage in my eulogy. The Sunday before, Michael had to leave worship early. He was having a difficult time breathing. What he didn't know then is that a respiratory infection had settled in his chest, signaling the beginning of his final chapter.

Until recently, Michael Beier had been a senior director of equity trading for a major bank in New York City. He loved his job, one filled with action and challenge. And he reveled in his family: his wife, Theresa; their little daughter, Carly; and baby Dustin on the way. On the treadmill at lunchtime one day, Michael's calf cramped up. After six months of tests—by an orthopedist, podiatrist, chiropractor, and three neurologists—Michael learned that he had ALS (amyotrophic lateral sclerosis), better known as Lou Gehrig's disease.

Michael soon began to dedicate this personal tragedy to the greater good. He became a vice president of the Muscular Dystrophy Association (MDA). Before long he was on the board of the famed Packard Center for ALS Research at Johns Hopkins. In 2001 he helped plan Wings of Hope, the MDA-sponsored reception that raised $320,000 for the center's research. The following year he chaired Wings Over Wall Street, dubbed by one writer "the Night of 1,000 Traders," bringing almost $2 million to the cause. "At first," Michael said, "I didn't set out to be a Christopher Reeve type and get so involved in organizations. But then I decided I should do something now, while I could still speak."

ALS is a devastating condition. The negative-print image of Alzheimer's, which takes away an often otherwise able-bodied person's mind, ALS traps a perfectly working mind in a disintegrating body. Michael was thirty-six when he learned he had it.

The week he died, Michael and Theresa gave me a book, beautifully bound and poignantly illustrated with family pictures, titled *I Love You Forever* by Daddy. Seizing this last chance to spell out his love clearly, Michael dictated the text during the last month of his life. It begins:

Dear Carly and Dustin,

This letter is so hard to write; it is one of the hardest things that I have ever done. Each time I try to dictate it, I become so choked up that I can't get the words out. It is so hard to think of everything I want to say. Since I've had ALS, I've done more thinking that I have in thirty-nine years. I've thought so much about doing this letter, but I have never been ready to say goodbye to my beautiful kids. There is so much that I want to say, and that I want you to know. So, I'll do my best to tell you some of the things I have been thinking about.

Since Carly's most vivid and Dustin's only memory of their father will be of him with ALS, he tells them stories about how he and their mother met, their courtship and wedding, their favorite vacations, the children's birth. "Your mother is and has always been the number one priority to me," Michael tells Carly and Dustin. "I hope that you understand how wonderful our relationship has been. It wasn't because I had ALS or was sick. The ALS never affected our love. In fact, it was a test and we came out winning. Before and after I got sick, our love has been strong. The only thing that has kept us together is love."

Michael goes on to compose a modern version of what in the Middle Ages was called an ethical will. In addition to a last will and testament distributing their property, medieval Jews occasionally passed on to their children a written bequest of their values. In sorting through my own family's papers, I came across such a will written by my great-great-grandfather, a Mormon bishop. Today, the AIDS epidemic in Africa is orphaning so many children that ethical wills are increasingly common. Often bound, as Michael's is, these books are filled with stories from the children's early childhood, which they otherwise might not remember, together with tips for living a good life, and sealed by expressions of love.

Unlike in my great-great-grandfather's ethical will and those of many medieval rabbis, no warnings are attached to Michael's gift. No "do this or else." No burden of guilt. As many parent-child relationships so sadly illustrate, love coupled with guilt forms an intrinsically unstable bond.

In *I Love You Forever*, Michael shares his favorite food (chicken parmigiana with spaghetti) and color ("Right now it's blue") and holiday ("Christmas because I love giving presents"). He tells his children about the movies and music he loves. And then he offers a few carefully selected and touchingly illustrated life lessons:

- Take care of each other.

- Walk away from trouble.

- Use your time in school wisely.

- Make sure you think before you speak.

- Always ask for help.

- Always eat the best part first.

He goes on to teach his children things he has learned about reading and money and friendship. About ALS and sickness and hard decisions. And about his growing faith in God. He also speaks to Carly and Dustin openly about death, assuring them that he is not afraid. He said the same thing to me the last time we met. Michael was not afraid of death, because he had made his peace with life.

A proportional relationship exists between the fear of death and the fear of life. The fear of death diminishes our trust in life by increasing our awareness of the risk of living. Diminished trust and an increased awareness of risk are two primary sources of fear's debilitating power. Having mastered fear, nearing his hour of death, Michael was able to open his heart fully. Many of us struggle to do the same, even years before our appointed time. Until we can embrace death as (along with birth) one of the two essential hinges on which life turns, we remain, at least to a degree, in hiding. Doors locked and windows shuttered, we are unable to let in joy and experience love.

It would be difficult to be as conscientious a parent as Michael was during the short time allotted to him as a father. But everything we really need to know is right there in the title of his book. By calling it *I Love You Forever,* Michael imparted the greatest of all truths, and therefore the greatest of all gifts, to his children: the wisdom that love, and only love, never dies. "I will always feel your love for me," he says in closing. "Always feel my love for you. With all my heart, Daddy."

The first public attention to ALS came in New York's Yankee Stadium, when Lou Gehrig announced to his fans that he had contracted ALS—a disease that was destined to be named after him. "Today I consider myself the luckiest man on the face of the earth," he said. "I might have had a tough break, but I have an awful lot to live for." I thought of Gehrig's words when I joined Michael and some twenty family members in his living room the morning of his final day on earth. He was in complete control of the situation. Giving us our marching orders for his funeral. Making sure that we were all taking care of one another. And asking for the Last Rites, which I, as a Unitarian, performed imperfectly. That was just the way he wanted it, Michael said.

Shortly before his own death, Gehrig reported with elation word of a new antidote that seemed to be working to arrest the rate of muscular degeneration. "I've got good news for you," he reported to his old friend Bob Considine. "Looks like the boys in the labs might have come up with a real breakthrough. They've got some new serum that they've tried on ten of us who have the same problem. And you know something? It seems to be working on nine out of the ten. How about that?" Talking with him further, Considine discovered that Gehrig was the one for whom the serum had no effect. "It didn't work on me," Gehrig admitted. "But how about that for an average? Nine out of ten! Isn't that great."

Again, the question to ask is not "Why?" "Why?"gets us nowhere. The only question worth asking is "Where do we go from here?" And part of the answer must be "together." Together we kneel. Together we walk, holding one another's hands, holding one another up. As for a life that ends too soon, in the eye of eternity the only lives that end too soon are those that won't live on in others' hearts.

*   *   *

From September 18, 2001, until the end of December (and occasionally thereafter), *The New York Times* published brief obituaries of men and women who died on 9/11. We are used to reading obituaries of the famous and infamous. These were of ordinary people, their lives both as alike and as unique as fingerprints.

And what stood out in these brief obituaries? Not worldly success, nor a list of noted accomplishments and positions. In almost every instance, what stood out was love given and received.

Scott M. McGovern

Just before bedtime, Ms. McGovern said, her husband would pick up Alane, the older of their two daughters, wrap her in a blanket and walk out to the driveway of their house in Wyckoff, N.J. "Where are you going?" Ms. McGovern would ask them. Scott would whisper back, "We're going to wish on a star."

Cora Hidalgo Holland

"I loved my mother's hands, her extensions of her soul," Nate Holland, now 19, said in eulogizing his mother. . . . "She had hands like silken clay, forever soft and always warm. When I was a child she would tuck me into bed and run them through my hair as we talked until I could talk no more. I would drift into sleep as her fingers floated across my scalp. The second that she withdrew her hand I would awaken, her rhythmic lullaby ending, but I would still pretend to be asleep."

David S. Berry

"It was raining stunningly hard, and all the kids, of course, were running around the house naked," Mrs. Berry said. "David was running with them. Water was just coming down in buckets, and they remembered how it was coming down the gutter, like a faucet. In playing with the children there was no distraction," she said. "He was nowhere but right there in the moment, right there."

Christopher C. Amoroso

The other night, after Sophia Rose Amoroso had her bath, she looked at her tiny hands, wrinkled from the bathwater, and told her mother, Jaime, "I have Daddy's fingers." . . . She will [also] always have the letter he wrote her when she was 10 weeks old: "Sometimes it makes me cry, as I am overwhelmed by the joy I've been given by you and your mother. I want you to know that I consider myself the luckiest man to ever walk the face of this earth. If anything were to happen to me, I could honestly say I've known true love and happiness in my life."

Each of these brief notices is filled with heart—heart as gratitude and heart as courage. Love conquers fear because it cannot die. Michael Tucker's obituary closes with "He was Michael, he was Mike, he was Tuck to his friends from school and he was Daddy, and he's still making us smile." In a memorial service for his two brothers, Keith and Scott, Todd Coleman said, "I will try to live my life in a manner that will be worthy of their respect and admiration. . . . Their memory reminds me that the world can be a wonderful place." On the day he was to die, George E. Spencer left a note for his wife on their kitchen counter: "Stop being critical of yourself," it said. "Enjoy life. Today is another day. Chance to live a little."

Eternity is not a length of time; it is depth in time. We enter and meet there through the sacrament of love. The *Times* death notices and Michael Beier's ethical will are testimony to the courage to love; each answers fear's no with love's yes.

Michael's funeral was a celebration. After watching a brief video highlighting his life, the entire congregation stood in applause. The truth, however, is that Michael *was* just a regular guy. That is what makes his courage so inspirational.

THE COURAGE TO BE

No one needs to try to be unique. Nevertheless, being who we are remains a daily challenge. The three things required—self-acceptance, integrity, and the courage to be—don't happen on their own.

Self-acceptance demands that we aspire to be, not disdain, who we are; it rejects disguise, knowing that it is neither helpful nor necessary. Integrity is oneness—being in harmony with ourselves and our neighbor. The courage to be is nothing more and nothing less than a fundamental affirmation of our own uniqueness, a uniqueness conditioned by the limits imposed by life and death. Practiced together, self-acceptance, integrity, and the courage to be lead to human freedom. In contrast, fear disguises reality, trades in duplicity, and rejects human limitations, thereby making freedom impossible.

Dr. David Kelley heads the psychological services group through which I run all my referrals for extended psychotherapy. If members of my congregation wish or need individual therapy or couples counseling—if they find themselves in trouble at home or at work or suffer from depression, anxiety attacks, traumatic stress syndrome, or any other acute or debilitating condition—I send them to David and he matches them with a professional. Many psychological conditions have an underlying biological basis, so the right kind of therapy can be a lifesaver. We can't pull ourselves up by our own bootstraps when they are broken.

I once asked David how he happened to choose his profession. He told me that as a boy he had been terrified by death and, accordingly, by life. In my discussion with David, I recognized again how closely related these two fears are. David told me that as a result of therapy, he finally made peace with who he was. After a particularly revelatory and healing counseling session, he walked out of the therapist's office suddenly free of the weight that so long had burdened his existence. Somehow he broke fear's logic—that life's limits are unacceptable. Accepting those limits, he was now free to accept himself and especially his fate. The enormous relief he felt, together with his gratitude for it, led him to a career helping others find liberation from their own crippling fears.

Insecurity tells us that we are inadequate; guilt, that we are flawed; worry, that bad things could happen; dread, that we have no control over our existence or our fate. As do the courage to act and to love, the courage to be answers fear's no with a yes. To illustrate how powerful this yes can be, even in the face of death, the most inspirational testimony I know comes from Socrates and Jesus.

Plato relates the trial of Socrates, which led to his conviction and death, in the *Apology,* a recapitulation of Socrates' defense. As is true of all classical "apologies," Socrates is not seeking forgiveness; he is boldly and artfully justifying his actions. He had been charged by the Athenian Council (their version of our federal courts) with "corrupting the minds of the young, and of believing in deities of his own invention instead of the gods recognized by the state." In a split decision, a jury of his fellow citizens condemned him to death. After completing his defense—contesting the prosecution's charges by dismissing their validity point by point—Socrates accepts the sentence the judges have laid down. "The difficulty is not so much to escape death," Socrates reminds them. "The real difficulty is to escape from doing wrong, which is far more fleet of foot."

In a worldly sense, Socrates has little that death can strip him of. "I have never lived an ordinary quiet life," he tells the court. "I did not care for the things that most people care about—making money, having a comfortable home, high military or civil rank." Furthermore, judging death itself to be either the sweetest sleep or transport to a better world where justice never miscarries, he declares himself not only unafraid of death but open to exploring its possibilities. At this point in his defense, Socrates turns to the jury and proclaims: "Nothing can harm a good man either in life or after death."

For Socrates, the courage to be is indistinguishable from integrity. As long as he remains at peace with his conscience, guilt can place no limitations on his freedom. To sacrifice his integrity would be much worse than sacrificing his life. Though accused of sacrilege, he can say (with death's nearness the guarantor of his honesty), "I have a more sincere belief than any of my accusers, and I leave it to you and to God to judge me as it shall be best for me and for yourselves." In death as in life, Socrates perfectly illustrates the courage to be.

*   *   *

For millions around the world, the greatest story ever told
is that of Jesus the Carpenter's Son. Yet it is a story without
any of the markings by which the world measures success.
No riches. No earthly power. Not to mention that the hero
dies young, branded a criminal and nailed to a cross. Yet all
of us, whether Christian or not, can draw meaning from his
life. His courage can sustain our courage and deepen our
understanding of the complex interplay among love, fear,
and freedom.

Jesus entered Jerusalem with fanfare, leading a band of
followers who believed that he was the messiah. Within a
week he was betrayed by one of his disciples, brought before
Pilate, sentenced, and crucified. His followers disbanded
and went into hiding, in fear for their own lives. His chief
disciple, Peter, forswore him three times rather than admitting to any knowledge of him. This is not the way the story
was supposed to turn out. By ancient tradition the promised
messiah, scion of David, king of the Jews, would march triumphantly into Jerusalem to be crowned. Apparently, this
was the expectation of many of Jesus' Palm Sunday followers. The problem is, their expectations had nothing whatsoever to do with Jesus' gospel.

Reminding us that the world doesn't owe us a living—
rather it is we who owe the world a living, our very own—
Jesus' good news celebrates the gift of sacrificial love. To
take his most challenging injunction, by loving our enemy
we give away our entitlement to revenge; we sacrifice our
pride. We also sacrifice our sense of entitlement and all the
pleasures that go with vengefulness, bitterness, and hate. Forgiveness, too, requires sacrifice. We must sacrifice self-
righteousness, our preoccupation with having been wronged,
and the advantage of holding another in our debt. Finally,

and most important, we must sacrifice our control over everything that lies beyond our power—including our control over others, over events, and over the future. Ultimately, the courage to be requires the courage to let go. Fear accompanies us all the way to the grave, but we needn't hold its hand or accept its cold comfort. The word *sacrifice* literally means, "to render sacred."

When most believers reach out to Jesus, it is to the fully human Jesus. His are hands we can hold. When tears well in his eyes, we know our own are blessed. The fear of Jesus is just like our fear. He worries. He wonders if he has done all he could to accomplish his mission, and at the end of his life, for one dramatic moment, he fears that he has failed, that everything was for naught.

We know that Jesus struggled with fear as he hung dying on the cross. It is written all over his last words. Jesus almost never quoted Scripture, but here we find him, at the hour of his death, quoting not the comforting Twenty-third Psalm but the starker Twenty-second—not "I shall walk through the valley of the shadow of death and fear no evil for thou are with me" but "My God, my God, why hast thou forsaken me? Why art thou so far from helping me?" Instead of the comforting words that usher in the close of the Twenty-third Psalm, "My cup runneth over," Jesus moans, "I thirst."

Where, then, in this drama is the breakthrough? Where does courage answer fear? It comes first when Jesus further says, "Father, forgive them, for they know not what they do." He thinks not about his own fate but about the fate of others. He returns to the very essence of his gospel—to love our neighbor as ourself. And also to love God. Jesus completes his surrender of self by placing his life in God's hands, saying, "Father, I commend my life unto thy spirit."

When we feel that we are alone, that God is not with us—when our heart is filled with dread about life or about death—we can take to heart the saving fear of Jesus, his own sense of abandonment by God, his all-too-human thirst. We can reach out as he did, not only *for* help—though that is a very fine thing to do— but *to* help as well. Letting go, Jesus recalled his own saving truth: love your neighbor; love your enemy; God is love; and love casts out all fear.

Promising to protect our hearts, fear closes them instead. Love will have none of this. "Fear not," the angel says to Mary as she is pondering the new life blossoming in her womb. "Fear not," he later comforts the shepherds who, watching their flocks by night, have been stunned by the brightness of a holy star. The same words echo throughout Jesus' teachings: "Fear not . . . fear not . . . fear not." And they echo as clearly in Socrates' defense, implicit in his diffidence toward death and in his intimacy with a trust and honor that no one, including the force of death itself, can ever strip him of.

After death our bodies may be resurrected. Our souls may transmigrate or become part of the heavenly pleroma. We may join our loved ones in heaven. Or we may return the constituent parts of our being to the earth from which it came and rest in eternal peace. About life after death, no one knows. But about this we surely know: there is love after death. Our actions invest life with meaning and purpose. And life itself, regardless of all limitations, is a gift. To embrace being alive and having to die and to do so with compassion and integrity is to practice the courage to be.

FREEDOM

TEN KEYS TO FREEDOM—
LIGHTENING UP

We are born free. To remain free, we have to win back our freedom daily—from institutions and individuals, including ourselves, that operate under fear's direction. The poet-philosopher Goethe summed up the height of wisdom in this ringing challenge:

Of freedom and life he only is deserving
Who every day must conquer them anew.

Peace of mind rests on freedom, but for us to secure that freedom, courage must contest fear's arguments whenever they are posed—which is almost all the time.

To answer fear's best arguments effectively, three strategies commend themselves. As easy to remember as they may be difficult to accomplish, each nonetheless lies fully within our power:

- Doing what we can.

- Wanting what we have.

- Being who we are.

Doing what we can focuses our mind on what is possible, no more and no less, thereby filling each moment with conscious, practical endeavor. Wanting what we have mutes the pangs of desire, which visits from the future to cast a shadow across the present. And being who we are helps us reject the fool's gold of self-delusion. It also demands integrity—being straight with ourselves and one another—which, in turn, requires a clear conscience. Shakespeare put it simply: "Virtue is bold, and goodness never fearful."

Freedom from fear exists only in the present. Conversely, fear invades the present from the future, especially when imagined trouble—worry about tomorrow, an awareness of all that lies beyond our control—dominates our thoughts. To overcome fear's seduction, we must therefore travel from where we too often are (trapped somewhere between past and future) to where freedom lives (squarely in the here and now). Among the many ways people manage to unlock the present, I have ten personal favorites, each of which has the power to spring fear's lock in an instant, almost whenever we choose to be free.

For the first of these, I echo G. K. Chesterton: "Angels can fly because they take themselves lightly." On the assumption that what works for angels can't help but be good for us, my first key to freedom is *Lightening Up*.

When we laugh we fill the present with joy, something that alone would make humor fear's sworn enemy. More specifically, lightening up is the best antidote I can think of for every kind of unnecessary fear. Levity addresses worry's tendency to obsess, scoffs at the demon of perfectionism, exposes (as our enemy, not our friend) the self-absorption that lies at the root of insecurity, and undermines dread's relentless fatalism. When we laugh at ourselves for abetting fear, it evaporates like a wicked witch in water.

Keeping my first key at hand throughout, I devote a chapter apiece to the other nine:

- *Practicing Thoughtful Wishing*. Wishful thinking trips us up so often that we may as well intentionally set out to be miserable. Better yet, we can turn wishful thinking inside out and practice thoughtful wishing instead— wishing to do what we can, want what we have, and be who we are.

- *Resetting Our Alarms*. Most personal alarm systems are far too sensitive for our own good. To reset them, first we have to admit the limits to our ability to avoid all danger, then decide how secure we really need to be. To guide us, we can turn to ancient wisdom in search for the golden mean between being reckless and overly cautious.

- *Posting a "No Vacancy" Sign*. Every time we invite the future into our lives, worry accompanies it. When we occupy the present fully, however, there is no room for worry. To it and the other unhelpful fears, we put out a "no vacancy" sign.

- *Unwrapping the Present*. The present is a gift. We can receive it only by wanting what we have. To want what we have is to unwrap the present.

- *Taking the Stage*. We act, therefore we are. Character is driven less by what happens to us than by how we respond. By taking the stage, we steal it from fear.

- *Acting on 60 Percent Convictions*. By doing what we can (no more but also no less), yet still making allowances for failure, we act on our faith, not our fears. We can do so with confidence because the faith we demonstrate is self-ratifying.

- *Remembering the Secret to It All*. The overexamined life is not worth living. When we feel singled out as life's personal target, the best thing to do is say to ourselves—not only about fear but about everything—"It's not about me."

- *Praying for the Right Miracle*. If we treat life like a lottery, we are playing the wrong game. There's nothing wrong with praying for a miracle. It works better, however, when the miracle we pray for can actually save us.

- *Letting Go for Dear Life*. The better part of valor lies in knowing when to hold on and when to let go. It takes courage to do both. But we secure ultimate freedom by letting go for dear life.

PRACTICING THOUGHTFUL WISHING

Until we learn to wish for the right things, what we wish for will only come true by accident. What's worse, if we wish for the wrong things, the fear of disappointment will dog us from one broken dream to the next. To escape repetitive disappointment, my second key to freedom turns wishful thinking on its head.

Prescriptions for happiness should come with warning labels. When they don't work (which is often), we feel worse about ourselves than before. They are like Trojan horses, beautiful on the outside but filled with enemy soldiers. Imagine bringing home some grinning guru's *Seven Surefire Steps to Happiness* from the bookstore. We curl up in our easy chair in anticipation of enlightenment, only to get hopelessly stuck on step two. It's like taking the cure and getting sicker.

Here are but a few of the more popular self-help bromides and favorite old saws: *Keep all your options open. Leave nothing to chance. Climb every mountain. Dream the impossible dream. Refuse to accept second-best. Don't take no for an answer. Treat your children like adults. Keep a stiff upper lip. Get in touch with your inner child. Expect a miracle. Don't stop thinking about tomorrow.*

One reason these seductive slogans tend to work better as songs than as strategies for living is that they leave us wanting to do what we can't, have what we don't, and be who we aren't. Each is an open invitation to insecurity, guilt, and worry.

Since the pursuit of happiness is almost guaranteed to make us miserable, we might just as well set out to be miserable in the first place. For instance, most of us have developed a surefire talent for undermining our confidence by selectively comparing ourselves with others. Insecurity absolutely thrives on this talent. Let's say we have a coworker who is enormously creative. Overlook that she has just broken up with her fifth husband, has a "little" problem with alcohol, and is on the verge of a nervous breakdown. Forget all that. Simply measure our creative capacity against hers and weep. Then there is that friend who is always the life of the party. We know how immature he is. No matter. He is always the life of the party. What's wrong with us? Why can't we be the life of the party sometimes? And how about our rich second cousin? Just look at him. He has everything anyone could want. Admittedly, we've never seen him smile and he barks at his dog. But how happy *we* would be with only half his money!

Not all of us are prone to this game, but most are. Selecting the finest traits and talents of everyone we know, we subconsciously fashion a composite ideal, measure ourselves against it, and come up wanting. It's insecurity's favorite trick. To accomplish it to perfection, ensuring that our heightened sense of inadequacy establishes a permanent residence for fear in our mind, we put all our friends' and neighbors' strengths together, then weigh our own in the balance and despair at our relative weakness, poverty, incompetence, and general all-around unattractiveness.

Fear loves nothing better than comparison. Once sufficiently insecure, we can then start feeling guilty. The quickest way to achieve this is by resolving to reform ourselves utterly and put our composite perfect neighbor to shame. To stay miserable, we must forget about the things we enjoy and tend to do quite well. We will never reach perfection by building on our strengths. So we tackle something for which we have no aptitude whatsoever, fixing upon *that* as our ultimate goal in life. Fear will cheer us onward, since each time we fail at achieving the impossible we feel even guiltier than before.

Conversely, we may have a quick temper. Or procrastinate. Or eat too much. These are things about which we can perhaps do something. To remain miserable, we must avoid taking action at all cost. Here is where worry comes in handy. Rather than taking action to correct these problems, we worry about them instead. While we worry, at the same time we rationalize our inability to address these issues, ascribing our powerlessness to fate or the damage inflicted by our parents. That's the way to stay miserable. We don't sew up our wounds. Instead, we lick them as if they were lovers or nurse them like babies. After all, if we were to tackle some aspect of our lives that we could, in fact, do something about, we might succeed, leaving our precious worries in the lurch.

Happiness doesn't follow when we long for what we lack—for things we have lost or shall likely never find. The past is over. What we pine for is probably very different in our selective memory than it was in reality. And longing for something we may find in the future distracts us from enjoying the present. Wishful thinking is both sloppy and sentimental. We should think to wish instead for things closer at hand:

- The courage to bear up under pain

- The grace to take our successes lightly

- The liberation that comes with forgiveness

- The energy to address tasks that await our doing

- The meaning to be found in giving ourselves to others

- The patience to surmount things that are dragging us down

- The joy to be gained in even the smallest tasks

- The pleasure of one another's company

- The wonder that lies between the sacred moments of our birth and death

I call this thoughtful wishing—wishing for what is ours, here and now, to have, do, or be.

Fear (the great champion of wishful thinking) tries to persuade us that such wishes are insufficient. Reject its counsel. With thoughtful wishes, the odds turn in our favor. In fact, we can't lose. It's like dreaming the possible dream. All we have to do is put our heart into it. With but the slightest cooperation on our part, thoughtful wishes always come true.

RESETTING OUR ALARMS

We can worry ourselves to death. My third key to freedom resets the alarms that trigger such worry—not to lower our sensitivity to the point that we place ourselves at risk, just enough that we aren't terrified for no good reason. We can't do this with fright: to eliminate fright's false alarms would destroy the entire system. But we can with the other fears. It's one thing to set off an airport security alarm because we forgot to take a crumpled gum wrapper out of our pocket, but when our inner security systems are this jumpy, they go off just as needlessly. To avoid harm, we may even put ourselves in harm's way, as a familiar children's story memorably points out.

It all starts with an acorn. Worry often begins with little more than a seed. This particular seed falls on Chicken Little's head, leading her to conclude that the sky is falling. "It scared her so much she trembled all over," the story goes. "She shook so hard, half her feathers fell out."

Whether sparked by legitimate fright or arising on its own in the mind's creative department, worry is contagious.

Once they hear that their friend has felt the sky falling, Henny Penny, Ducky Lucky, Goosey Loosey, and Turkey Lurkey respond to Chicken Little's alarms. They are "beside themselves" (a telling turn of phrase), racing down the road to find the king in hope that he may save them.

In their panic, Chicken Little and her fellow cluckheads create one. They shoot straight into the welcoming arms of Foxy Loxy, who recognizes good fortune when it falls into his lap. "Follow me, and I'll show you the way to the king," Foxy Loxy says. Playing the piper to their fears, he leads them into the woods straight to his lair, "and they never saw the king to tell him the sky was falling."

On September 11, 2001, the sky actually did fall, leaving three thousand lives crushed beneath it. The unthinkable proved possible—extending fear's compass while adding to its persuasiveness. To each new danger we encounter, however, we must not forget to add the peril posed by fear itself.

After 9/11, several parishioners came in to discuss their heightened worry about living in New York, a completely reasonable concern (or so it seemed at the time). Everyone's anxiety had ratcheted up a notch. Orange Alert expressed not only an official state of readiness but also, for many, a personal state of mind.

The problem with worry is that its object casts a shadow that blocks out all other considerations. So I asked them a question or two. Had they considered that New York is now freer of violent crime than most other large cities in the country? Or that our teenage children are safer from car accidents than are teenagers elsewhere, since they don't need cars? Had they weighed the danger of driving to wherever they might consider moving—Maine or Oregon, perhaps? It could be as dangerous as living for quite some time under Orange Alert.

Fear is more likely to move trouble from one burner to another than to turn down the flame. The changes we make in our lives because we are inspired by something positive are much more likely to prove successful. Besides, wherever we manage to escape to, we must bring the cause of most of our troubles—ourselves—with us. Not to mention that safety is an illusion. The worries we leave behind will be replaced by new, unforeseen worries. Wherever we live and no matter how carefully, disaster is fickle. It has no respect for places or persons.

I received a call from one woman in my flock whom I thought had reached the breaking point between staying in New York and keeping her sanity. When she told me, a little breathlessly, that she had decided to remain in the city, there was a lightness in her voice that I hadn't heard for a long time. The clincher, it turned out, was a phone call from the Midwest. She had just finished talking with a close friend who had fled Manhattan for a sleepy town right outside Kansas City. If any place was secure from terrorism, this was it. The night before, twisters had decimated Main Street and residential areas less than a mile from his new home.

"I'm feeling a little better about New York," she said with a laugh.

"If you begin to waver," I replied, "I have this great book about Los Angeles. It's filled with every imaginable natural and unnatural disaster—earthquakes, brush fires, mudslides, and even drive-by shootings. You'll absolutely love it."

Many familiar stories—whether fables, biblical tales, or literary classics—explore the nature of fear. In one of his

Canterbury Tales, Geoffrey Chaucer relates the cautionary story of Chanticleer, a chickenhearted yet vainglorious barnyard cock. One morning Chanticleer wakes up trembling after a terrible nightmare. His hen, Dame Pertelote, asks what's wrong.

"Oh!" Chanticleer replies, shivering. "I had the most terrible dream. As I wandered down by the wood a doglike beast sprang out and seized me. His color was red, his nose small, his eyes like coals of fire. It was dreadful!"

Ashamed to discover that her husband is a chicken, Pertelote takes him to the woodshed, admonishing him for being frightened by a dream. "You must be brave to keep my love," she tells him.

His manhood questioned, Chanticleer determines to play the rooster. But not without a lingering pang of doubt. He has heard of dreams that later came true.

The following dawn Chanticleer is back performing in the barnyard as usual, flapping his wings, throwing his head back, crowing exultantly. His dream forgotten, he no longer feels afraid. Then along comes Reynard the fox—chickens and foxes often show up in each other's stories—flattering Chanticleer by comparing his song not unfavorably with the magnificent song of his father before him, who, Reynard recalls, "closed his eyes when he sang." Taken in by this flattery, Chanticleer stands up on tiptoe and closes his eyes, readying himself to burst forth in the most glorious of refrains. Seizing the opportunity, Reynard pounces, seizes Chanticleer by the throat, and races toward his den for an early breakfast.

The barnyard explodes in alarm. Geese honk; pigs squeal; the poor widow who owns the little farm races from her porch to pursue the fox, accompanied by a pack of barking dogs. Reynard speeds away with Chanticleer between his teeth. Chanticleer may have been foolhardy and vain, but fright focuses his wits. Since it was flattery that got him in this mess in the first place, he employs the same trick to get out of it. "How swiftly you run!" Chanticleer manages to gasp. "They'll never catch you. Have some sport with them."

Flattery plays not only to insecurity but also to pride (grounded more in insecurity than we may imagine). Snapping at the bait, Reynard opens his mouth to taunt his pursuers, and Chanticleer flies free. To reclaim his loss, the fox sweetens his tune again, begging Chanticleer's pardon for frightening him and promising a treat when they get to Reynard's home.

"No, no," Chanicleer replies. "You will not catch me again. A man who shuts his eyes when he ought to be looking deserves to lose his sight entirely."

The moral of this tale and that of Chicken Little are not as different as they may at first appear. The moral of Chicken Little is not "never be chicken." It is "think before you squawk." Crying wolf, Chicken Little overlooks a waiting fox. Had she not literally frightened herself and her friends to death, the fox would have had to look elsewhere for supper. The moral of Chaucer's tale is "Think before you crow." Chanticleer manages to wriggle off the fox's plate, but only when he finally finds a prudent balance between being too chicken and too cocky.

In ethics, the golden mean for correct behavior falls equidistant between extremes, the right amount of any given quality perceived as ethically superior to too little or too much. Generosity, for instance, is the golden mean between miserliness and profligacy. Aristotle introduced the golden mean to Western philosophy 2,500 years ago. Weighing fear according to this ideal, the preferred alternative to panic is not fearlessness but prudence (the halfway point between the two). The word *prudence* today suggests fear, but originally it signified "right thinking." Numbered among the seven classic virtues, it meant knowing the good and acting accordingly. In terms of the familiar Serenity Prayer—"God grant me the serenity to accept the things I cannot change, courage to change the things I can, and wisdom to know the difference"—prudence is the "wisdom to know the difference." So understood, far from being a drab virtue, prudence invites us to be bold, not timid, as long as we aren't foolish.

Security is not a golden mean, but one end of a continuum that extends all the way to untrammeled freedom on the other. In this sense, security and liberty are opposites. Objects that are secured lock into place; they cannot move. Before resetting our alarms, we must therefore decide just how safe we wish to be, never forgetting that security itself is a form of bondage. Both security and bondage entail a loss of freedom.

In our search for the right level of security, there are national ramifications to consider as well as personal ones. To obsess over threats to safety while ignoring threats to liberty demonstrates as little enlightened self-interest as does a person who thinks nothing about borrowing logs from the walls of his home to replenish his supply of firewood. As the house grows draftier, in order to keep the fire burning brightly enough to make up for the lost heat, he must take more and more wood from the walls. Tending his hearth, he destroys his home.

Since we can purchase no security whose warranty will not one day expire, wisdom counsels lavishing at least a little security in exchange for liberty. Once we as a nation have done all the obvious and sensible things to protect ourselves against another terrorist attack, each additional fraction of protection exacts a proportional sacrifice of freedom. And not only freedom. When our alarms warn us only against threats that imperil our safety, they fail to alert us to dangers that may jeopardize our humanity. "Whoever fights monsters should see to it that in the process he does not become a monster," wrote the philosopher Friedrich Nietzsche. "When you look long into an abyss, the abyss also looks into you." In reminding his fellow Americans that the only thing we have to fear is fear itself, President Roosevelt sought to make us less vulnerable to our enemies, not more like them.

POSTING A "NO VACANCY" SIGN

Since unwarranted fear always visits from the future, we free ourselves from it by fully occupying the present. Employing my fourth key to freedom, we post a NO VACANCY sign outside the door of our mind.

A man pulls into his driveway. Before entering the house, he walks over to a large tree in the front yard, places his hands on one of the lower branches, bows his head, closes his eyes for a moment, and then walks up the sidewalk toward the front door.

"What were you just doing?" his neighbor calls across the fence.

"That's my worry tree," the man mysteriously replies. "When I come home after a hard day, rather than bringing my worries in with me, I hang them there." At further urging, he explains that his worries had become a distraction. He wanted to be sure his family got the attention they deserved during the few hours they were all together. So he found a way, every night when he got home, to remind himself of what really mattered—his family, not his worries.

"Does it work?" the neighbor asks.

"You won't believe how well," he says, shaking his head in wonder. "When I pause on my way to work to collect my worries from the evening before, more often than not they are gone. I ignore them for a few hours and they vanish into thin air."

Contrast this useful sleight of mind with its alternative—bringing worry home. Not only does it come with a ton of baggage, but before we know it, worry has taken over the entire premises.

Worry multiplies when we obsess over it. Conversely, it disappears when we direct our attention elsewhere. The same holds true for most other fears. They wander off when deprived of attention. One thing fear can't get around is a NO VACANCY sign. The sign must be for real, because we can't fool fear—not for long, anyway. Our home must be fully occupied, which means we must be occupied as well, not preoccupied or otherwise distracted. Remember, fear will keep knocking, and it holds a standing reservation for the first opening.

Redirected attention is not the same thing as inattention. Denial and escape may promote the illusion of dislodging fear, only to help it grow stronger. For instance, we may think we are drowning our troubles in a few drinks or by flipping through the channels until, exhausted, we fall asleep. Temporarily submerged, they only seem to disappear. In fact, they are happily occupied elsewhere. By going into hiding ourselves, we give fear the run of the household.

Once we recognize fear as a visitor from the future, the trick is to occupy the present completely, leaving our worries on the worry tree. This is more difficult than it sounds, because worry does everything possible to hold the door to the future open, abetting entry by enlisting powerful allies—desire, disappointment, guilt, insecurity, and dread.

Desire and disappointment empty the present of value;

we end up longing for what we lack. Guilt looks forward too in a way, leaving us fearful of being caught. Insecurity knocks us off-balance precisely because we are *pre*occupied—living, literally, not in this moment but in the very next—always about to embarrass ourselves or expose our inadequacies. Dread takes the future (from death on back) and darkens the present so completely that hope is extinguished.

One key to fighting fear is to divide and conquer, breaking it up into manageable pieces. For this reason, I am a great fan of lists. My favorite comparative list matches up things that are haunting us against those for which we are grateful. Drawing up a list of this sort can be illuminating. For instance, if we kept a record of all the things we fret about during the course of a day, would it be longer or shorter than our list of the day's accomplishments? Assume that it is longer. If we saved both lists for later review, we would realize that most of our apprehensions had long since evaporated even as our accomplishments remained for us to build on.

I once asked a young woman who turned to me for help to draw up just such a list. She couldn't think of a single amen since breakfast to balance against her column of complaints. I ended up referring her to a psychotherapist, but on the face of things, she seemed less depressed than defeated, less disheartened than cynical. Talking further, we discovered one possible reason for her malaise. She was afraid of good feelings because they would not last. She hesitated to invest herself fully in anything—from her job to her latest relationship—that might reap major personal dividends, for fear that from the moment she really cared, her life would go bust. She was the Little Engine That Couldn't.

"I think I can't, I think I can't," the Little Engine moaned as it slid back down the hill.

Maybe she was born with a tilt in this direction. "Nature" does that to us sometimes. We have no power over the genes we inherit. A fortunate few are born sunny-side up, others over easy; lots of us are slightly scrambled, some are hard-boiled. We are also products of all we experience, some of which can be so destructive that it leaves permanent scars. "Nurture" can reflect a lack of nurture, producing tough eggs as well as unusually fragile ones.

Nonetheless, fear is a tireless inventor. By way of apprehension, it invents future danger and brings it home for us to worry about. Apprehension is the future's dark counterpart to nostalgia, the art of selective memory, which leaves an empty place where recalled happiness once made its dwelling. Whether nostalgia sells the present short or apprehension does, the place we occupy is equally bereft of joy. When we shutter our mind against the very people and things that might temper our worries and disappointment, the present is condemned.

David is a young man in my congregation. He entered the world months before he was expected and needed major surgery the day he was born. After eight full weeks in the intensive care unit, his grandparents dubbed him "the Mighty David," and he lives up to his name. Not that it's been easy. Over the succeeding fourteen years, he has had numerous operations and been bedridden for months at a stretch. And then, when David was ten, his mother died of cancer.

At my church we celebrate what we call Coming-of-Age Sunday, when our young people share their personal "credos." In his credo, or statement of faith, in recalling the difficulties he has had to surmount, David said, "From these

setbacks, I learned many lessons. First, I learned to perse-
vere. When obstacles are coming toward you, you must take
a deep breath, stare right at them, and be tough. Second, I
learned to be patient. It took a long time for me to get my
health stable, and I had to learn to be tolerant of many
things. Third, I learned love and support. For my whole life
of ups and downs and trials and tribulations, love and support were, and are, always around me."

David's credo showed more maturity than many a college
application essay. He had turned his pain into wisdom.

> I think about the future and think about what I will be
> doing years from now. Honestly, the fact that I have
> no idea what will happen to me in the future frightens
> me. I am the type of person who likes to know what
> will happen if I engage in something. I rarely appreci-
> ate surprises. That is why I am trying harder to grasp
> control over my life and be more responsible, so I will
> be headed in the right direction in the future. I have
> had trouble disciplining myself at times, and my
> schoolwork can be inconsistent at times, even though
> it turns out well in the end. As I am getting older I am
> working toward being more engaged in my school-
> work and more focused on other types of interests,
> such as tennis and guitar. I have a whole life ahead of
> me and I have to try to love and enjoy life as much as
> I possibly can.

David has known many troubles. That life doesn't come
with a warranty is painfully obvious to him. The future
scares him, as it does us all, precisely because none of us
can control or predict what will happen to us and to the

people we love. Yet at a young age, David has begun to figure out that we can influence the future in only one way: by engaging the present with our full attention and energy. A game of tennis locks David into the moment. So does his guitar. Or an evening spent cracking the books (promising that tomorrow's test will be slightly less daunting). David is courageous both in confessing his fears and in addressing them.

By picking up any of the projects that give our lives meaning and devoting our full attention to them, we too can occupy the present more fully. To this end, it is useful to break our lives into projects. The parent project. A project at work. A favorite hobby. Even, perhaps, an old-friend reclamation project—all we have to do is pick up the phone. The moment we do, we put out a NO VACANCY sign to fear. There is no room for it right now. We have better things to do.

Edward Everett Hale, longtime chaplain of the U.S. Senate and author of *The Man Without a Country*, once said: "Never bear more than one trouble at a time. Some people bear three kinds—all they have had, all they have now, and all they expect to have." It doesn't need to be like this. Hanging our worries on the branches of our worry tree, we can instead look forward to the present. We may even safely indulge in a bit of nostalgia for the present as it passes. Then today becomes not only tomorrow's good old day but also its very own.

UNWRAPPING THE PRESENT

The present is not only a dimension of time—it is also a gift. Each moment we live is the only one we are given to redeem, for the past is over and the future remains uncertain. When we unwrap the present (my fifth key to freedom), we enter a world that is completely ours. We receive the gift of life.

If you are a parent, one way to unwrap the present is to read to your children. As with every pastime that connects our hearts, it makes them stronger. Pay attention to your child's favorite book (or remember your own favorites when you were a child)—it may be quite scary. We begin dealing with our fears when we are very young by experimenting with them in safe ways. Reading a fairy tale is a perfect way to be scared and safe at the same time.

When I was a boy, my favorite books dealt with fear in a different, equally effective way. They made fun of it.

Edward Bear, better known to generations of children as Winnie-the-Pooh, is the resident philosopher of Pooh Corner.

Among my favorite memories as a young child is snuggling into bed with my father on Saturday mornings for him to read me one of A. A. Milne's Pooh stories. My father sometimes laughed so hard that he cried. To a six-year-old boy, such parental abandon is pure bliss.

Because Pooh's dearest friend, Piglet, is such a timorous soul, fear is a major theme in *Winnie-the-Pooh* and its sequel, *The House at Pooh Corner*. Worry, for example. Pooh and Piglet's hunt for a Woozle illustrates worry's logic to a tee. Walking around a tree, Pooh looks down to discover a pair of tracks before him, indicating perhaps the presence of a Woozle. He follows these tracks only to discover, upon circling the tree again, that a second creature has joined the first. The scent of growing danger both attracts and alarms Piglet, who—reluctant though curious—joins Pooh in his quest. When he does, the beasts they are following multiply.

"Do you see, Piglet? Look at their tracks! Three, as it were, Woozles, and one, as it was, Wizzle. *Another Woozle has joined them!*" This revelation, and the peril it represents, is too much for Piglet, who suddenly remembers that he has some pressing errand to run and hightails it home, "very glad to be Out of All Danger again."

On another occasion, Piglet and Pooh manage to trap themselves in a pit they have dug in which to capture a Heffalump. Should they now lure this terror of their imagination into the pit, the dread beast would instead capture them. "What happens when the Heffalump comes?" asks Piglet. Pooh may be "a bear of little brain," but he always applies what mind he has to constructive problem solving. "Do what you can" is Pooh's mantra. So, to Piglet's great encouragement, Pooh hatches a plan. If a Heffalump should chance along, the two of them would say, "Ho-*ho*." Should this jaunty display of pluck fail to neutralize the Heffalump— should he respond, say, with a "ho-*ho*" of his own—Pooh would then hum. Confused by so nonchalant a response to his fearsomeness, the Heffalump could not help but doubt his power. Pooh then would be in the position to point out triumphantly that rather than the Heffalump capturing *them* (as appearances together with his strength advantage might suggest), the poor beast had instead fallen into a trap built by them expressly to capture *him*. Rather than fear mastering them, they would master it.

"Pooh! . . . You've saved us," Piglet squeaks, launching into a heroic reverie in which, having cowed the dread Heffalump by humming, Piglet himself has become a profile in courage.

My father's favorite chapter in *Winnie-the-Pooh* was the story of Eeyore's birthday. Eeyore is a donkey who is subject to depression, forever pessimistic and forlorn. As if to compound his misery, Pooh and Piglet each independently botch the presents they had intended to give him for his birthday.

Running to make sure he is not late for the party, Piglet trips, falling on the balloon he was bringing to Eeyore and bursting it. Upon receiving the balloon's remains (a "small piece of damp rag"), Eeyore inquires what this curious gift might be. "A balloon," Piglet improbably suggests.

"Balloon?" says Eeyore. "You did say balloon? One of those big coloured things you blow up? Gaiety, song-and-dance, here we are and there we are?" Upon discovering that the balloon was red (Eeyore's favorite color) and had once been about the size of Piglet (Eeyore's favorite size), the woebegone donkey feels almost as miserable as Piglet himself.

Then Pooh comes along with his gift, a jar of honey that on his way to Eeyore's party, in a moment of self-forgetting abandon, Pooh ate. Wishing Eeyore many happy returns of the day, Pooh sheepishly presents him with a useful empty pot in which to put things.

Animated by an unaccustomed shiver of excitement, Eeyore declares, "I believe my Balloon will just go into that Pot."

"Oh, no, Eeyore," Pooh protests, starting to explain that a ballon is much too large to fit into a pot.

"Not mine," Eeyore responds proudly. Before long he is "taking the balloon out, and putting it back again, as happy as could be."

These two truly pathetic birthday presents might easily have reinforced Eeyore's fatalism. Instead, they bring him unexpected satisfaction. Unwrapping the present, he finds himself wanting what he has.

We can also have everything we could possibly ever need and still come up wanting. Sometimes, to distract people I am counseling from their self-absorption, I introduce an embarrassing chapter from my own life. Let me share with you the cautionary story of the Christmas Child.

When I was a boy, as is the case with many children, Christmas was the high point of my year. Not its spiritual high point, I'm afraid—its material high point. Until I was nine I was the only child in a large, doting family. As such, I served an important Christmas function. After another year of solid middle-class semipuritanical austerity, all that pent-up parental and grandparental Christmas spirit needed an outlet. It needed a child. My great aunts, too, and honorary uncles, not to mention the mysterious cousins who gathered around the family hearth each year, might have missed Christmas entirely without my eyes to look at it through. It was the perfect gift exchange. I gave everyone my big round eyes, and they gave me presents. In concept, Christmas in my grandparents' home on Idaho Street in Boise was the perfect win-win holiday.

Like many of us, I sometimes diminish the present by

romanticizing the past. Still, I remember enough of what *really* went on long ago in my grandparents' house to recognize that Christmas in concept did not extend to Christmas in reality. I was not wholly to blame for this. At least, I trust that is the case. But since most of the adult hijinks sailed over my head, my memory conspires to place me not only at center stage every family Christmas but also at the center of the annual family Christmas catastrophe.

This catastrophe was as predictable and inevitable as my grandmother's pumpkin pie. I would ask for things for Christmas. My doting family would take my list and add to it, until on the night before Christmas our delightfully decorated tree was almost obscured by presents of every size, weight, and description, the great majority of which (detective work revealed) were tagged for me, the household Christmas Child.

After dinner on Christmas Eve, the Christmas Child would dutifully and to great approbation put on a puppet show or some other entertainment appropriate to the holiday and then be whisked upstairs to bed so that the adults could devote themselves to the construction of his Major Gift.

Here the charade began. I only pretended to go to bed, cracking open the door so I might pick up snatches of adult conversation and then, at what appeared to be critical moments, sneaking down the stairs and peeking through the banister. Lying wide awake in bed, I was sick to my stomach in anticipation of what the morning would bring.

I don't know how long I slept. Very little, I am sure, because I didn't actually fall asleep until all the grown-ups were in bed, freeing me to sneak downstairs into the living room to check out their handiwork and poke and shake the packages that had materialized during my supposed slumber. I remember how mysterious and still it was, just the embers from our coal fire to guide me through the perfectly prepared living room to the altar of presents in front of a grand, darkened, expectantly bedecked Christmas tree.

I also know that I was the first one up in the morning. As the only child in the family, this was my prerogative—to demand the attendance of all my courtiers at the very crack of dawn, which I remember impatiently waiting for before crashing into my parents' room to announce that *Christmas Had Come*. How painful this must have been for them I know only from later experience, when my own children were young. Today, with all of them in the throes of late adolescence, even on Christmas Day I can't get any of them up much before noon.

When I was a child, at dawn the Christmas morning drama would begin to unfold. The center of everyone's attention had had next to no sleep and was sick to his stomach with excitement and anticipation. The adults, as best as I can recall, were good sports about this. From later experience I know, however, that Christmas morning is when parents who are fortunate enough to be able to do so realize that they have overdone Christmas. I can well imagine how these dozen or so adult relations must have cringed while pondering the general decline in morality as, with growing horror, they watched the Christmas Child rip through one package after another, hardly bothering to discover whom each was from.

Finally—and here is where Christmas really got ugly— the Christmas Child, for one reason or another, suffered a complete meltdown. Provoking this (though little provocation was needed), in the crush of toys and the chaos of torn paper, I would step on or, in attempting to put together, mangle what was at that very instant my favorite, most important, Absolutely Irreplaceable Gift. The rest of this story is simply too painful to relate, but I can assure you, it cast a pall over Christmas that would not lift until I had a long, restorative nap.

I have no idea how often this melodrama repeated itself, though it remains—filed under "guilt"—-vivid in memory. Fortunately, for the sake of my young soul and the integrity of Christmas itself, my infant brother became the Christmas Child when I was nine, cousins began to have children, and—without a featured role—I started taking the whole thing a lot less seriously. Perhaps I began to see Christmas through my little brother's eyes. All I know is, over time, the less Christmas had to do with me, the better it got.

Fear visits from the future not only in the form of apprehension but courtesy of expectation as well. Expectations exist to be disappointed. They give us one more thing to worry about. Even when met, they can throw us off-balance. My early expectations for Christmas were enormous. And by any objective measurement, they were always surpassed by my family's remarkable largesse. Nevertheless, because my expectations were not fulfilled, I ended up feeling disappointed. The adults, in turn, anticipating how grateful and happy I would be when I unwrapped my gifts, couldn't help but have their own expectations diminished by the reality of Christmas morning. Their expectations, too, led to resentment. Unable to look into the mirror and embrace ourselves and one another as we were, we all measured the reality of our lives against the dream of their incomplete fulfillment.

Harry Potter and the Sorcerer's Stone features a magic mirror. Actualized in its reflection are the fondest dreams of anyone who gazes into it. Harry's friend Ron sees himself being crowned the Quidditch champion. Harry sees himself united with his parents, both of whom are dead. When the wizard encounters Harry gazing into the mirror, imagining the joy of having what is not his to have, he tells him, "It is bad for you to spend so much time in front of that mirror."

And then the wizard actually says something very wise. He explains to Harry that only when we look into this mirror and see ourselves as we actually are can we be accounted truly happy. Nostalgia leads to heartache; dissatisfaction to envy; expectation to disappointment.

Eeyore's birthday party demonstrates the very opposite of disappointment, dissatisfaction, and nostalgia. Only by unwrapping the present—our fondest wish being to have what is ours, do what we can, and be who we are—will our wishes surely be fulfilled.

The various animals who frequent Pooh Corner each experience one version or another of this epiphany. But the true sage in *Winnie-the-Pooh* is Pooh himself. The essence of Pooh's sensible approach to life—and fear—is summed up in a single observation. On their way to visit their friend Owl for tea, Pooh and Piglet find themselves buffeted by a great windstorm. Pooh holds Piglet's hand tightly. "Piglet's ears streamed behind him like banners as he fought his way along." When the two travelers finally reach the shelter of the Hundred Acre Wood, rather than expressing gratitude for having escaped the real peril of being blown away, Piglet interjects into the equation a new cause for alarm. "Supposing a tree fell down, Pooh, when we were underneath it?"

To which, after careful thought, Pooh replies, "Supposing it didn't."

TAKING THE STAGE

Worry and action are opposites. Insecurity, guilt, and dread, too, stifle action and, in turn, are stifled by it; it is impossible to fret and act at the same time. For this reason, my sixth key to freedom, taking the stage, counters fear in a direct and effective way.

"I think, therefore I am," the philosopher Descartes memorably proclaimed. To whatever extent this observation may be true, it is not useful. We are known by our actions, not our thoughts. Life is not a spectator sport, but performance art. How we act during its pivotal scenes, not what we think, tells the story. "In the beginning was the deed," Goethe said. In other words, "I act, therefore I am." The theater brings this truth to life—the word *drama* means "action."

It was Shakespeare's Jacques in *As You Like It* who said, "All the world's a stage, / And all the men and women merely players." His dark soliloquy echoes elsewhere in Shakespeare. King Lear laments to his jester, "When we are born, we cry that we are come / To this great stage of fools." Macbeth calls each of us "a poor player / That struts and frets his hour upon the stage," our life, "a tale / Told by an idiot, full of sound and fury, / Signifying nothing."

If such is the nature of the show, why even bother acting? First, because cynical Jacques, broken Lear, and the weak Macbeth, if not demonstrably wrong, are no more than 100 percent half right. We do age; our health fails; we die. And we certainly play the fool at times. But are we all idiots, our lives signifying nothing? It doesn't feel that way to me. In fact, from both experience and observation, I know—and you know, too—that how we act can make a dramatic difference in the way our life plays out. So what if some people read their lines and hit their marks in a way that suggests little room for improvisation (literally, "the ability to improve"). Have we not each seen the very opposite as well— brave souls who, reimagining their entire lives by displacing fear as their director, took a bad script and tore it to pieces?

If the story of our life is turning out poorly, we don't have to despair. We serve on the creative team that is writing it, with principal responsibility for character development. We also have more power to vitalize a dull tale or reverse our hero's fortunes than we may imagine. I have watched individuals turn their lives around during the course of a single life-wrenching, heart-stopping scene.

Mary, a relatively young (though life-battered) member of my congregation, dramatically molded a new life by breaking the grip of a gambling obsession. For years she had begged her way back from the brink, but finally she fell over it. Her disease left her bankrupt, jobless, homeless, separated from her husband, estranged from her children, and facing criminal charges for graft.

It was at this point in her story that I first met with her—in the hospital after a suicide attempt. Never have I counseled anyone who felt more humiliated. Guilt possessed her entire being. She was also terrified of change, especially of entering a rehabilitation clinic. Yet she mustered the courage to act. In one final, life-saving gesture, she incarcerated herself in a sixty-day lockup and came out a free woman. Two years later her children have taken tentative steps toward reentering her life. She has steady work, is about to move out of the halfway house assigned by the court and into her own apartment, and is paying back her old employer on a ten-year schedule. Sound grim? On the contrary. For the first time in her life, she told me recently, she is free from the hammerlock of fear. At the same time, she is running one of our church social-outreach programs, taking care of her health, and living (as all twelve-steppers must) one day at a time.

We can't make our lives problem-free, but as Mary did, we can script them in such a way that they are solution-driven. How we coscript our drama makes a world of difference in how it plays. This holds true whatever scenes the fates may cast us in, as Mary certainly learned.

So did Alison. I first met Alison when she was three years old. The following autumn I officiated at her dedication service (a Unitarian christening). I got to know her family well. Her mother, an indispensable member of the congregation, was always ready to perform any task that needed doing. Her brother—today a lawyer—was slow to develop his motor skills and the focus of his parents' concern. And her father suffered from a debilitating and progressive heart condition, finally dying when Alison was fourteen years old.

Two years later Alison was diagnosed with fibrosarcoma, a rare and heretofore incurable cancer. For the next thirty months, wearing a little red bandana, she trudged in and out of New York Hospital, the doctors trying one experimental therapy after another, her body ravaged by disease, radiation, and chemotherapy. Her mother, a nurse, was her daughter's dauntless champion. She oversaw Alison's care with tenacity. When her doctors said that for Alison to live, they would have to amputate her arm, her mother swept her off to Houston to a doctor who agreed that doing so would only traumatize, not save, her. Another way had to be found. As for Alison herself, between long hospitalizations she made regular visits to the cancer ward, not only for treatments but to visit her new friends—to comfort them and give them courage, to make them laugh—as, one by one, too many of them died.

Meanwhile, Alison sailed through high school. No other child diagnosed with the same cancer had survived so long. Yet during her senior year, Alison and I didn't talk much about cancer. We talked about the high-school church group, which she, in essence, led. We talked about college. We probably even talked about the weather. You wouldn't have known how sick she was or the fears she must have harbored about having a future at all. Ten years later, now officially cured, Alison is a minister herself. But she had always been a minister. Throughout the years of her illness, she ministered to others. That was how she held her fears at bay.

If you didn't know anything about Alison or her subsequent accomplishments as a young adult, the plot of her early life would read like a melodrama. Her beloved father, struck by one crippling blow after another, dies. She then contracts a rare form of cancer, her life hanging in the balance for years. Whenever it seems that she may be getting better, she suffers another setback. It's like the perils of Pauline on the iceberg. As for poor Nell being tied to the train tracks, look at Mary's story. How many times can one person be rescued from the same fate?

The difference between melodrama and drama is both simple and telling. It has nothing to do with plot. Both drama and melodrama can feature a plot with many twists and death-defying turns. But in melodrama, as the plot develops, the characters remain static. Pauline and Nell are as two-dimensional after their ordeals as they were before. Mary and Alison were not. In the course of the human drama, whatever the plot may be, character develops.

Suffering doesn't always build character, but it certainly gives us a chance to display it. Two different people can respond to the same events—the same melodramatic plot—in radically different ways. One is estranged from life and hope; the other grows in empathy and understanding. The former gets lost in the thickets of self-absorption and succumbs to her fears. The latter discovers that what's happening is actually not about her but mirrors instead the depth of the human condition.

During times of crisis (those times that we fear the most and that produce the most occasion for fear), the courage we demonstrate can liberate us from fear's grip at the very moment such freedom seems impossible. Crisis is not something that befalls us. In Greek drama, the word *crisis* literally means "decision." Whenever life springs a trap, events follow from the decisions we then make, how we respond driving the plot of our lives as often as it builds character. A strong imagination carries events; it doesn't succumb to them. Crisis in the theater is that moment when the hero makes his or her fateful choice. Dramatic action follows from decisions we make as decisively as it does from the things that befall us.

Complementing this notion, the Chinese ideogram for *crisis* is composed of two word pictures—*danger* and *opportunity*. With every danger comes an equal opportunity. Often we don't perceive the opportunity. It lies hidden in danger's shadow. We will never perceive it as long as we remain in bondage to anxiety and fear. But it is there.

*   *   *

Some directors evoke the widest possible emotional range from their actors by stressing "emotion-memory." They ask their players to recall what they have felt before in similar situations, in order to keep feeling alive and emotion vivid. Other directors believe that true emotion can be found in the script itself, in the experience of the character whom the actor portrays. In either case, the only way for actors to portray their roles authentically and well is by "feeling" their way.

Like stage actors, we too must feel our way. But one feeling can block us from exploring and experimenting with our loftier emotions—stage fright. Fear ties us up in knots and pulls them tighter, entangling our lives and their plots. Rather than developing, our story remains basically static from one scene to the next—as in a melodrama. In effect, when we cede the stage to fear, our lives live us.

It doesn't have to be this way. In classical drama, the word *denouement* means, literally, "untying the knot." Mary finally untied the knot that was strangling her. So did Alison. When they did—as so often happens when we take the stage—they stole the show.

ACTING ON 60 PERCENT CONVICTIONS

How do we know that the action we take will make our lives better, not worse? Quite simply, we don't. If we did, action would be a no-brainer and courage unnecessary. Action requires courage because fear never stops reminding us that:

- We could be wrong.

- We could fail.

- Even if we are right and don't fail, the process of getting from where we are to where we want to be will whip up so many more reasons for worry, guilt, and insecurity that we could spare ourselves a ton of trouble and embarrassment simply by staying put.

Some years ago, undecided on which path to follow at a major junction in my life, I came up with the 60 Percent

Solution. You have a decision to make. It may be an important decision. Should you marry him or not? Should you quit your job? Adopt a child? Come out of the closet? Move to Vermont? I would counsel against doing all five of these things at once, but even a single major decision can paralyze us. What if we make the mistake of our lives?

This is where my seventh key to freedom comes in handy. We are leaning 60-40 in favor of doing something. If we go ahead, we act on a 60 percent conviction. With the odds in our favor, on a 60-40 bet we go for it, mindful that we may be making a mistake. Presuming an average capacity for judgment and our fair share of luck, if we act regularly on 60 percent convictions, a like percentage of our decisions (often more, as we'll soon see) will turn out well. As for the rest, we can either write them off as the cost of doing business or—the spiritually finer approach—add them to our balance of humility.

Contrast this with the 40 Percent Solution. Here, though we're still leaning 60-40, we act on our 40 percent fear, not our 60 percent faith. Dreading the consequences of doing the wrong thing, we don't lay a bet even when the odds are in our favor. Unlike Yogi Berra, when we come to a fork in the road, we *don't* take it. We dare act only on a lead-pipe cinch or with a money-back guarantee. Because real life is far from cinchy and tends not to return our money, over time we act ever more infrequently. We are completely safe from failure, of course. No one has ever missed a shot he didn't take. But absolute safety has its consequences. It's like practicing being dead.

A few dangerous souls escape this problem entirely. Unlike 60 percenters who act on their faith and 40 percenters who—dallying from one expiration date to the next—act instead on their fears, these folks are the 100 percenters. They trumpet and act on their convictions with absolute certitude.

They are obviously right, and anyone who thinks otherwise ought to have her head examined. Whenever someone with whom I agree is 100 percent positive that he is right, I am tempted to change my mind immediately.

These 100 percenters are as impervious to worry as character-disordered individuals are to feelings of inadequacy. For the rest of us, however, a 40 percent window of opportunity is all fear needs to display its complete set of wares. Since we tend to avoid pain more readily than we seek pleasure, we are more wary of failure than enticed by success. That is why fear can champion a weak position so persuasively.

One of my most memorable pastoral encounters pivoted on a 60-40 decision. An insurance executive in my congregation—successful, strikingly handsome, in his mid-thirties—was in love. Chris told me he wanted to get married, but he was afraid. He might not be the right person for his prospective fiancée, or she for him, or some especially grim combination of the two. Chris didn't actually think this was the case. Of all the women he had dated, Claudia was the first he had really fallen for. They had dated for more than a year and knew each other well. She was clearly the one for him—he knew that. On the other hand, how could he be certain that he wasn't making a dreadful mistake?

At the end of our third session, having fussed over the same tea leaves many times, I gave Chris four choices and invited him to pick one: get married and be grateful; get married and regret it; remain single and be grateful; remain single and regret it.

Understandably confused, he said, "I don't get it. What do *you* think I should do?"

"Be grateful," I replied.

The day of their wedding arrived. Chris looked paler than usual but still dashing in his tuxedo, and Claudia was gorgeous. At the end of the ceremony, after I pronounced them husband and wife, Chris embraced me. At least I thought that was what he was doing. When the embrace grew heavy, I realized that he had fainted dead away in my arms. After laying him out in the aisle, I rushed to the church office, where a World War II–issue first-aid kit had languished, unopened, in a drawer for forty years, waiting for precisely this moment. Breaking open an ancient glass vial of smelling salts, I brought Chris back to life. Together we signed the marriage license. I began secretly to wonder whether it was time to retire my shingle and stick to preaching.

The story continues, as life does. One life-changing 60 Percent Decision leads quickly to another. A few weeks later Claudia and Chris came in together for counseling. She was pregnant, they told me, but without the level of delight one would anticipate from those who come bearing joyful news. As it turned out, Claudia wasn't quite as young as Chris had been led to believe. The night before (in what we can surmise was a fascinating conversation) she had confessed to being not in her early thirties, as he thought she was, but forty—a youngish forty to be sure, but forty nonetheless. Among other things, this bit of actuarial data had an impact on the odds of her bearing a healthy child, placing amniocentesis at the top of an almost endless marital agenda.

Claudia is Roman Catholic. She told Chris that although she was happy to undergo such a procedure, her faith required her to have the child even if amniocentesis showed that the fetus was damaged. So that piece was easy. I suggested that she not undergo the procedure, since it posed a slight danger and the results would have no bearing anyway. After an hour's oblique discussion about trust, forgiveness, and other relevant virtues, I sheepishly passed them over to a splendid marriage counselor. Two weeks later Chris called to thank me and to say good-bye. His company was moving him to Chicago. I wished him all the luck in the world (some of which he would clearly need) and then spent a few minutes cringing in consultation with my conscience.

After a decade during which I heard nothing from them, last year Claudia and Chris showed up one Sunday in church—together with their three children, running from almost ten to about six years old. They were showing the kids where Mommy and Daddy had gotten married. And then off they flew to pack as much of the city into a single afternoon as they possibly could.

Chris and Claudia didn't fill me in on any of the particulars of their story from the time we lost contact, when their world was falling apart, until now. They really didn't have to. Clearly one 60 Percent Decision had led to another, and, on balance, things had worked out just fine.

Even when the 60 Percent Solution is more like a 90 Percent Solution (with nine reasons to do something and only one weighing against it), fear plays every trick imaginable to get us to devote as much attention to that single concern as to the other nine arguments combined. We may end up not acting at all, on the one chance out of ten that something might go wrong.

Conversely, you would think that the diciest decisions we make would turn on 51 Percent Solutions. This is not always the case. Both doubt and faith are self-ratifying. My favorite action hero, the Little Engine That Could, succeeded only because he willed his decision into a reality. In our lives, too, the real test lies not in making it up to the top of the hill but in deciding to climb it in the first place. For those who dare to act, even a 51 Percent Solution turns out on average far better than the odds might suggest.

In the end, acting on 60 Percent Convictions has less to do with accepting being wrong 40 percent of the time (as important as that may be) than with acting on our faith. Doubts are self-ratifying. So are beliefs. The trick is to turn the one into the other. Even with our most agonizing doubts, when we finally muster the courage necessary to act, what may have begun as a 60 Percent Decision seems almost fated in retrospect. Just ask Claudia and Chris.

One final thought about these two. When agonizing over his decision, Chris was adrift in a sea of self-absorption. But when he finally took the stage and acted on his 60 Percent Convictions, his story got more complex and, accordingly, more fascinating. It wasn't any longer just about him. It was about him and Claudia, and then about the two of them and their children. Once we are no longer the subject of every sentence, fear can't modify our lives as trivially as it once did. Which leads us to my eighth key to freedom, remembering the secret to it all.

REMEMBERING THE SECRET
TO IT ALL

Fear is a flatterer. "It's all about you," it says. This is a lie. After thirty years of ministering—looking beyond my own mirror into the world's—the one thing I've discovered is that "it's *not* about me."

Mirrors play a role in many well-known stories. Aesop tells the fable of a dog with a bone in his mouth who walks past a pond and sees a dog beneath the surface holding a bone at least as big, maybe bigger. Suddenly envious of the reflected dog's bone, he opens his maw and bares his teeth to attack, leaving both him and his reflection boneless. Aesop's dog is so into comparison that he loses what he has in a failed attempt to get something more.

Mirrors can confuse us in other ways. By studying ourselves in them too intently, we become self-conscious and insecure. Or, as with Harry Potter's mirror, we lose our lives in wishful fantasy and, twisting who we are into a dream of all we're not, overlook the many things for which we might be grateful. The Greek story of Narcissus offers yet another take on the dangers of a mirrored image. Narcissus falls in love with his reflection in a pool, wastes away on the banks of the water, and dies. One variant of this tale has the love-struck boy drown while attempting to embrace himself. We could add another: Narcissus is so paralyzed by fear—worried about his future, tortured by guilt, self-conscious about his inadequacies, dreading his fate—that he drowns in his reflections. Drowning in our reflections is a perfect metaphor for self-absorption.

Fear advises us to worry, feel guilty, be insecure, and dread the future, precisely because everything *is* about us. Everything is conspiring against us, or is our fault, or is our problem. I heard the Reverend William Sloane Coffin say once that "there is no smaller package in the world than someone who is all wrapped up in himself." When we are all wrapped up in our worries, guilt feelings, and insecurities, we have no room to maneuver. We can't lighten up, because matters are too grave. To unwrap the present is no answer, because the present is dreadful—it is all we can do simply to escape from it. As for what we have, who would want it? And we can't act, because nothing we do ever turns out right. Life is stupid. We are worthless. Or victims. Or the subject of a vast, hidden conspiracy. When we feel like this, there is only one way to improve the picture: remove ourselves from the middle of it.

Meredith is a doctor. She was a member at All Souls when I arrived, but although she came to church almost every Sunday, I didn't actually meet her for several years. Later she told me that she would slip into the last pew after services had started and then leave right before the benediction, to limit the danger of direct human contact. Meredith is a brilliant woman. She graduated first in her class at Stanford Medical School. She is also cripplingly shy. Because of her insecurities, she opted for clinical medicine, doing research by herself or with one or two others in a lab, a comfort zone in which she could work without too many emotional distractions.

Meredith first called more than twenty years ago to suggest that the church organize an outreach program for the people in our neighborhood. It must have taken her days to work up the courage to make that call. I said, "Great!" and put her in charge. She went on to set up several volunteer programs and was elected to the congregation's board of trustees. Today we have more than thirty social service programs and social justice groups. Not only has Meredith had a hand in several of them, but in recognition of her leadership, she went on to be appointed to the board of a major national service committee, which she eventually chaired.

Shyness—a common and debilitating form of insecurity—was Meredith's main problem. Meredith is still shy. I expect that she overcomes fear every time she rises to speak, yet she always speaks with clarity and eloquence. I asked her once how she did it. How had she moved from the back pew to the pulpit? How was she able to overcome her shyness to address a huge audience, chair an important meeting, or speak at a press conference? "Because," she said simply, "I'm never thinking about myself when I do these things."

As long as Meredith remained self-conscious and consumed by insecurity, she was hamstrung. The last thing in the world she wanted to do was draw attention to herself. She couldn't let go of her concern for others, however, and finally had to step forward on their behalf. The courage to act came from the fact that what she was doing was not about *her*, but about *them*. The more she devoted her attentions to her neighbors' needs, the less time she had to think about her own inadequacies. At the age of fifty, she married for the first time. She is now an active stepgrandmother, her life an ever-expanding circle. When Meredith turned away from her own mesmerizing reflection, it disappeared.

Conversely, when we obsess about our fears, the bravest among us will feel cowardly. This truth is summed up brilliantly by L. Frank Baum in *The Wonderful Wizard of Oz*. You can't just rent the movie; you have to read the book. Fortunately, it is a splendid book, perfect for grown-ups who have forgotten what it feels like to be a child.

In the book, when the Cowardly Lion and his four traveling companions happen upon a deep, impassable ravine blocking their path to the Emerald City, they realize that the only way they can continue their journey is for the Lion to jump across, carrying the others over on his back one by one. "I am terribly afraid of falling," the Cowardly Lion confesses to his companions, "but I suppose there is nothing to do but try it. So get on my back and we will make the attempt." The Lion springs back and forth across the ravine, carrying the Tin Woodman, the Scarecrow, Dorothy, and Toto to safety on the other side.

Whenever danger visits, the Cowardly Lion, though frightened to death, always and promptly does the courageous thing. In his dramatic showdown with the terrible Kalidah monsters—twice his size with bearlike bodies and tigers' heads—the odds against him are fearsome. "We are lost," the Cowardly Lion concedes, "for they will surely tear us to pieces with their sharp claws. But stand close behind me and I will fight them as long as I am alive."

True to form, the Lion declares himself ready to die defending his friends. Not that he looks into the mirror afterward and sees the reflected glory of his courage. Mirrors confuse us because they contain our *reflections* as well as our *reflection*. Self-interpretation colors what we see. So it is with the Lion. Against all evidence to the contrary, knowing that he is afraid confirms his belief that he is cowardly. He fails to recognize that courage has nothing to do with fearlessness. As noted above, courage is possible only when fear is present. Courage is not the elimination of fear, but the mastery of it. Mastering his fear, the Lion shows as much courage as anyone could possibly hope for. But because he is so wrapped up in all four kinds of debilitating fear—worry, guilt, insecurity, and dread—he remains fear's captive.

The Wizard of Oz ends with the pilgrims receiving from the phony wizard something they already have. The tenderhearted Tin Woodman gets his heart; the wise Scarecrow his brains; Dorothy returns home simply by clicking together the heels of her shoes; and the Lion receives a vial of courage. Everyone but the Lion goes on to live happily ever after.

We know this because Baum wrote many sequels to *The Wizard of Oz*, permitting us to follow our heroes through their later adventures. During a long life, the Scarecrow misses no opportunity to boast of his wit. And the Tin Woodman never stops showing off his heart. But the Lion loses his newfound courage almost as quickly as he attained it. Having been given what was theirs already, not only do the others now have what they want but they also want what they have. The Lion, however, remains as insecure and unhappy as ever. Every time he encounters a new danger, he is a scaredy-cat. And he hates himself for it.

One sequel recounts Dorothy's return to the Land of Oz and reunion with her old friends. Upon hearing the Lion still referred to as "cowardly," she protests with all her might. "But the Lion is not really cowardly," Dorothy exclaims. "I have seen him act as bravely as can be."

"All a mistake, my dear," the Lion interrupts. "To others I may have seemed brave at times, but I have never been in any danger that I was not afraid."

To which stouthearted Dorothy replies, simply and truly, "Nor I."

To liberate our lives from self-absorption, I have found three practices to be of particular value. Easy to remember, because each begins with an *e*, they are empathy, ecstasy, and enthusiasm. The literal meaning of each word contains its key. *Empathy* means, literally, "to suffer or feel within another." *Ecstasy* means "to stand outside ourselves." And *enthusiasm* means "to manifest the god (*theos*) within us."

Empathy is deep compassion. It is what inspired Meredith to face down her shyness and act, refusing to let her self-consciousness stand in the way of her conscience. How this works is really quite simple. By shouldering another's burden, we shift weight away from our own.

Far from being as self-indulgent as it sounds (an impression strengthened by *ecstasy* being the name of a prevalent and dangerous party drug), ecstasy takes us outside ourselves as well. Directing the mind away from close and continual inspection of our frets and grievances, ecstasy lifts us from our familiar haunts to life's inner and outermost horizons, where we can soar free from fear's limitations. When we stand outside ourselves, fear no longer circumscribes our existence.

Enthusiasm is exactly what the word says—filled with holy energy. If empathy and ecstasy remove us from fear's circle of power, enthusiasm fills that same circle so completely that no room remains for fear to set up its altar. Rapt, energetic involvement—in a book, game, or project— is one expression of enthusiasm. Spontaneous laughter is another.

It takes courage to laugh, especially when the things we

are struggling with are no laughing matter. The most healing aspect about the courage to laugh is that it keeps us from attaching additional strings to our troubles, no matter how serious they are. The journalist Linda Ellerbee memorably attests to laughter's healing power when she describes enduring the experience of a double mastectomy by calling laughter "the mother of courage."

Whether leavened by humor, lifted by contemplation, or lightened and expanded by neighborly concern, life opens up the moment we stop defining (and restricting) it on our own narrow terms. Once we understand the secret to it all—that "it's not about me"—we no longer cast fear's shadow.

How liberating this is. Rising out of our self-pity, we shake off the temptation to whine, "Woe is me!" and "Why do these things always happen to me?" Rather than wondering why we don't have what she has and can't do what he does and can't be who they are, we take the opposite tack. We do what we can, want what we have, and accept who we are. The pond grows so still that we can see beyond our own reflection to the trees and clouds and birds and sun. And when night finally falls—which it will, sooner than we imagine—we see all the way to the stars.

PRAYING FOR THE RIGHT MIRACLE

It is human nature to pray for miracles, so much so that some of us think to pray *only* when nothing short of a miracle can save us, a net to break our fall or an angel to sweep down and catch us in her arms. The Russian novelist Ivan Turgenev went so far as to claim that every time we pray, we pray for a miracle. "Every prayer reduces itself to this," he said: "'Great God, grant that twice two be not four.'"

Sometimes twice two is *not* four. We have all known such miracles in our lives. A loved one awakens from a year-long coma. The cancer riddling a friend's body goes into sudden complete remission. Such things happen just often enough that it would be foolish not to throw a Hail Mary pass with two seconds left and one's life on the line. There is no shame in this. When the bombs come hailing down, an atheist has the right to blurt out, "God save me," from his foxhole. Whether or not God takes a hand in arranging the shrapnel, the atheist may miraculously emerge unscathed, which is certainly worth the intellectual compromise of a final desperate prayer.

To pray for such a miracle on your average Tuesday, however, is a different matter entirely. Such prayers may be answered, but the answer won't be yes. It will be "get real" (until fear whispers that we mustn't get real, because reality is precisely our problem).

There are dozens of ways to make up for this or that human deficit and thereby start balancing our book of life. We might begin by writing a few of them off—accepting those things about our lives that will continue to be what they are. Then we can chip away more profitably, with patient persistence, at more tractable troubles. Fear counters by reminding us that none of the little things we may do to improve our lot will make much of a difference. Besides, change is difficult. Miracles aren't. They take care of everything, without our having to lift a finger. Nothing can rescue us from a bind quicker than an escape fantasy. All we have to do is squeeze our eyes tight—little stars will dance inside our head. Millions of them perhaps. Look: This week the cash jackpot stands at 92 million dollars.

There we have it. The lottery. If we are really lucky, not only will we win, we won't even have to share it. (Have you noticed that the first thing we do upon dreaming of winning the lottery is to hope that no one else selects the right number?) We could win, you know. Somebody will. Whoever wins will beat no less daunting odds. Yet even this stroke of absolutely brilliant fortune won't take us off the hook. Perversely, the way the lottery tends to work, even the lucky people who win may turn out to be miserable.

According to those who have followed up on lottery winners' lives, if we think our family is dysfunctional now, just wait until we win the lottery. At least when people die sitting on a fortune, they aren't around to observe how their family behaves. Evidently, winning the lottery big is like going to heaven and finding the place full of creatures from that famous bar scene in *Star Wars*. Before we know it, we become one of them: shifty, furtive, paranoid, grasping for gold straws. Even our closest friends will not be above suspicion. So we exchange them for a new set of friends: accountants, investment advisers, lawyers, and bodyguards. Not only that, but years later, after our new spouse has left us and we file for bankruptcy, the little debts we had accumulated before we got lucky will pale in comparison with those that remain in the wake of our misspent prosperity. In short, winning the lottery big could completely wreck our life.

Since we are *not* going to win the lottery (a safe bet for almost all of us), such misery is moot. Besides, instead of throwing away our money, we can get a free ticket anytime we like for a miracle that really can save us.

To pray for the right miracle is easy. If healthy, for instance, pray for health. Anyone who is ailing will remind us what a blessing health is and how rarely we think to give thanks for it while we are fortunate enough to possess it. There are millions of couples who can't conceive children, so we should always pray for children if we have them, no matter how much trouble they may cause. And for parents. Parents, too, cause trouble, but without the miracle of having them, we wouldn't be around to complain. We might also pray for any of the miracles of sight, hearing, smell, touch, and taste that we are blessed with; millions of people aren't, you know. As for our problems, why not pray for the sympathy of those who are concerned about our plight, whatever it may be? What could be finer or more welcome than to receive the love of everyone who loves us?

We needn't wait for a miracle to experience the miraculous.

Life itself is a miracle. Our very being is predicated upon almost impossible odds, odds infinitely more daunting than winning the lottery. Go back to the beginning of human history: all our ancestors lived to puberty, chose the only mate they could have chosen for us to exist, made love at the only possible moment, and united the only possible sperm and egg to keep our tenuous prospects alive. Then go back another billion years, all the way to the ur-paramecium. And billions of years before that, hedging the earth's bet on the combustion of gasses and the pinball of stars. A single, unbroken thread connects us to the very moment of creation. The universe was pregnant with us when it was born.

Do we ponder such things? Or do we instead ask ourselves, "What did I do to deserve this?" and then, losing hope the minute life tempers our optimism, pray not to awaken to the miracle that is ours—that is us—but instead to be saved by a miracle that will rescue us from what is by replacing it with something that is not.

"There is nothing that God hath established in a constant course of nature," writes John Donne, "but would seem a Miracle, and exercise our admiration, if it were done but once." Take something as unexceptional as summer, a miracle parceled out to us only a limited number of times during our brief lifetime. If we were to taste but once of summer, of sultry days and verdant trees, of ice-cream trucks and frilly frocks, would we not be amazed by how miraculous summer is? Would we not embrace both June and one another, saying, "Look! Summer. Can you believe it? It's a miracle."

Dreams don't need to be impossible. To climb one mountain in a lifetime is a wonderful thing. The joys of imperfection beat the burdens of perfectionism any day of the week. And whenever it pops up on the calendar, today has more promise than yesterday ever had or tomorrow ever will. In fact, it's an honest-to-God, blow-it-away miracle.

LETTING GO FOR DEAR LIFE

Flying home from anywhere, my heart catches when I look down on New York City, by night or day as beautiful a sight as I can imagine. It is almost impossible to witness the dreamscape of Manhattan from above without being at once awestruck and humbled, words that, in one sense, are each other's opposite.

Through my airplane window, I always search for All Souls, the church I have served for the past quarter century. Twice I thought I saw our steeple from my window, a tiny pin in a cushion of needles. On the clearest day with the most perfect angle, you have to know exactly where to look and then believe—not know—that you have seen it, one of twenty thousand towers composing perhaps the most spectacular skyline in the world.

Now I also look for the World Trade Center, knowing—not quite believing—I shall never find it again. I try to remember exactly where it was, giving ballast to lower Manhattan and far more imposing than any steeple. The true temple of this commercial metropolis, its ghost remains to haunt our

reflections. The Twin Towers are as humbling in their ab-
sence as they were awesome when present, as eloquent a
symbol of transience today as they once were of perma-
nence and power.

If pride is the number one sin—and medieval theologians
were almost surely right about that—then humility must be
the number one virtue. When it comes to fear, it is certainly
among the most functional. We have little control over so
many of the things that may endanger or diminish our lives.
To worry or feel guilty or inadequate about things we cannot
change is not only dysfunctional but also, in a strange way,
prideful. When we play God—doing what we lack the power
to do and being who we lack the power to be—like the tragic
heroes of old, we invite nemesis or, at the very least, let fear
rule our destiny.

Sometimes the better part of valor is to embrace what is,
however unwelcome it may be. Even after a catastrophe, we
can find ways to want what remains, replacing the unhelpful question "Why?" with the more promising "Where do we
go from here?"

There used to be a point system (employed by some as a di-
agnostic tool and by others as a party game) that assigned a
certain number of stress points for things like moving, losing
a job, the breakup of a relationship, an illness, or a death in
the family. During the brief time this point system enjoyed
favor as a party game, I remember joining with a group of
stressed-out friends to compete over which of us could tally
the most points. When someone broke a hundred—and was
therefore, for all practical purposes, dead—we had a winner.
Since this unfortunate person had lived not only to tell of
her death but also to laugh about it, the rest of us would
raise our glasses in wonder and admiration.

We shouldn't have been so surprised, either by her display of courage or the gallows humor she employed in recounting all the things that were happening to her. What the point system failed to take into account is that we almost always cope better when our entire world falls apart than when only a single part of it does. The reason is quite simple. When everything goes wrong, it is impossible to blame ourselves. Fear wants us to take credit, but the most self-absorbed among us has a hard time feeling responsible for the multiple catastrophe life has visited upon us. For the same reason, the aftermath of shared tragedy is remarkably free of emotional pleading. Few individuals act out or demand special attention. It is as if everybody's windows fly open simultaneously and a great gust of wind blows all the petty scraps off our collective plate. That we perform better (and often feel better about ourselves) during a crisis than we do on any average day should tell us something—how unnecessary a burden the fear we lug about with us from one day to the next truly is.

Frank, a nonagenarian in my congregation, tells me of how little fear he sensed, within himself and around him, during the six months that he, his wife, and a thousand others lived in a Quaker-run refugee camp at the beginning of World War II. In March 1939, Jewish refugees from Holland, Poland, France, and Czechoslovakia, with only the clothes on their back, were housed for six months in Broadstairs, a seaside town in the south of England. Frank contrasts those months to the years he served on the faculty of a prestigious medical school. In this academic bastion, fear had erected a fortress, students and professors alike struggling daily with professional worries, feelings of inadequacy, and the ghost of perfectionism.

The school was not unusual in this regard: fear sets up shop on most campuses, as it does in hospitals, businesses, even churches sometimes. As I said at the outset, fear is quick to "institutionalize" itself. It thrives wherever hierarchy exists, for hierarchies produce tension—between professor and student, boss and worker, parent and child. What was unusual enough that Frank still ponders it with awe is how a thousand people who had just lost everything short of their lives could live together in such amity and good humor. I have noted several times how fear trades in comparison—in "Who has what?" and "Who has more?" In Broadstairs, comparison was basically impossible. All the markers of distinction had been blown away. People had nothing but their freedom and one another. Things that mattered less or over which they no longer had controlling influence, they could only let go.

Reflecting back on our own experience of terror, we should not be surprised to have witnessed a dramatic rise in civility and expressions of mutual concern in New York City on September 11 and over the weeks immediately following. When catastrophe strikes, no one is singled out for special mistreatment; all within the circle of tragedy are one. Placed in dramatic perspective, personal feelings of guilt and inadequacy pale in comparison and, for all practical purposes, vanish. When they do, we become a part *of*, not apart *from*, the world we inhabit. This was certainly evident in New York. The sound of honking disappeared almost entirely. In elevators people asked absolute strangers (such as their upstairs neighbors) if they were okay or if they had lost anyone. The moment we recognize our own tears in another's eyes, our tears no longer blind us. Grief loses its isolating power and becomes instead a symbol of shared humanity.

It bears repeating: the opposite of love is fear, not hate. When we open our heart, love loosens fear's grip, even when fright has thrown us together. Overweening self-consciousness, ineffectual worry, and moral perfectionism are always silly, but only rarely—when we can't help but be conscious of more important things—do they fully seem that way. I observed the same phenomenon two years after 9/11 during the East Coast power outage. When the lights go out, who cares what we are wearing?

The dust that covered thousands of New Yorkers when the World Trade Towers collapsed obscured all marks of distinction: race, economic status, faith. We got a rare glimpse of how much more alike we are than different, our lives equally precious and equally fragile (something we can see at any time, but so rarely do). After 9/11, to the extent that any one of us was inadequate, we were all inadequate. No one could think that what was happening was all about him or her. There was even less *legitimate* reason for feeling guilty, because, unlike what often happens when a city's police force is diverted from its regular beat, in New York crime plummeted during the fall of 2001. Even the criminals were chastened. As for the kind of guilt that is sponsored by a fussy conscience, in the face of real crime and real tragedy, such guilt is exposed for what it truly is: a luxury.

We would be masochists to welcome disaster. Disaster doesn't build character. There simply isn't time. It does invite us to perform at our best, however—and later, to remember what that feels like. In the wake of 9/11, it took real work to remain spoiled and self-absorbed. We pooled our tears rather than wallowing in them. When we pool our tears, they do us all a world of good. When we wallow in them, we drown alone.

What do you worry about most? Is it your children? Or maybe your parents, suddenly like children in their dependency on you? Is it your health—a disease or condition that you have now or fear contracting? Or the health of a loved one? How about death—or does the pain and possible bondage associated with dying worry you more? Holding on for dear life sometimes permits a display of courage, but so does letting go for dear life. Precisely because fear always accompanies us on the journey from certainty to uncertainty, at certain twists in the road giving up on what can't save us (and also on what we can't save) is sometimes the only way to let go of fear's hand.

To release our father as he is dying—to tell him it's all right, that we love him and he can go now, freeing him from a hopeless battle by giving him permission to die—requires a kind of saving courage. Letting go of our children, as all parents must, into a frightening world, left to their own devices and to make their own mistakes, that too takes courage, even though we really have no choice. Then to celebrate them for who they are, not lament who they are not, giving up dreams for them that were ours to begin with, not theirs—this takes courage as well. It requires letting go, ceding control that was never ours to exercise in the first place. We can do this begrudgingly, regretfully, and plaintively, or we can do it with grace, wanting what we have, not lamenting what we lack. The results will be almost the same in either case. Our parents will pass on, and our children will leave home in pursuit of their own lives and dreams. The only difference is that fear will not preside over each departure and love will be free to reign in its stead.

However hard we may try to hold on to things we cannot keep, it avails us nothing. Here wisdom teaches us to let go in order to move on. At times of crisis, we must take a fearless inventory, holding on to what we can and letting go of what we must.

Finally, when it is our time to go, we have the same choice. After doing what we can to extend our useful life, we can choose to float on the outgoing tide or thrash about to keep from going under. Letting go for dear life is letting go of fear. In a final expression of love, we accept and bless the one condition that was placed upon life's gift and offer up our heartfelt thanks.

THE *FREEDOM FROM FEAR* BOOK CLUB

RESOURCES FOR COURAGE

To extend the conversation we have been having, I've created what I call the *Freedom from Fear* Book Club. You can join by yourself or bring along your friends—they too struggle with fear and seek courage. Along the way, you'll get to read some wonderful books.

For sheer pleasure and the simple good of our souls, I can think of no more fulfilling project than to pick up one of the classics. Great literature contains one example after another of beloved characters rising to life's occasion. More specifically, many of the classics illuminate the nature of courage in memorable and helpful ways.

I'm going to suggest that you begin with three novels: *To Kill a Mockingbird*, *Robinson Crusoe*, and *The Little Prince*. Even if you've read them before or think you know what they're about, read them again. One thing linking the three together is that—like Harry Potter—they each connect the adult and the childhood imagination. This is why their treatment of fear is so universal. They build bridges between past and present, childhood and adulthood, fear and courage, over which anyone can cross.

We tend to read the classics when we are in school, then never go back to them. It's different to read a book because we want to, not because we have to. The joy of rereading a classic (or reading for the very first time a story with which we are familiar) comes from knowing firsthand what the author is really talking about. Having enjoyed and suffered a wider range of true-life experiences than we had when we were in our teens, we are touched more deeply by stirring examples of the courage to act, love, and be. At the same time, opening our eyes as wide as they were when we were younger, we see things anew that we saw clearly once but have forgotten.

In my introductions to these three novels, I highlight issues that we have been grappling with throughout *Freedom from Fear*. *To Kill a Mockingbird* delves deeply into all five types of fear. *Robinson Crusoe* explores the three modes of courage. And *The Little Prince* illustrates my ten keys to freedom.

Further to expand our compass, I include summaries of seven noted works on fear by contemporary authors, books I have found to be of great use. Several of these books have won a wide readership, and for good reason. Others should be better known than they are. I hope my brief summaries interest you sufficiently that you turn to the books themselves for their many valuable insights.

I close with a brief study guide to assist book-group leaders in directing discussions of *Freedom from Fear*, and also to help individual readers reflect more deeply on its contents. Join with others to talk about your fears. It will give you courage. As important, it will help you put your fears in perspective. (If you come up with a sixth fear or find that my categories don't work for you, that's great, too. You might even let me know. Or share your own story about overcoming fear. I can be reached at revchurch@aol.com. I'd love to be included as an honorary member of your *Freedom from Fear* Book Club.)

CLASSICS IN COURAGE

To Kill a Mockingbird
Harper Lee

Maycomb, Alabama, 1933. The Great Depression has hit bottom and is resting there. Our narrator, Scout—the spunky, intellectually precocious daughter of Atticus Fitch, a local public defender and state assemblyman—reports that despite bone-crunching poverty, there existed a mood "of vague optimism for some of the people: Maycomb County had recently been told that it had nothing to fear but fear itself."

Since fear itself runs rampant in this rural southern hamlet, courage is the subtext for Harper Lee's beloved *To Kill a Mockingbird*, voted by America's librarians as the best novel of the twentieth century. The racially charged story of an innocent man's trial and unjust conviction for rape, no novel since *Uncle Tom's Cabin* has left such a strong imprint on the nation's moral imagination.

By accepting the town judge's request to defend Tom Robinson, a poor laborer, Atticus finds himself in danger. The townsfolk of Maycomb—and even his sister—turn on him for "betraying his race." When bigotry and fear collaborate (as they do here), they function almost like fraternal

twins. On the surface they may look different, but by nature
they share several basic traits. Like fear, bigotry is contagious. Also like fear, it grows in virulence as it spreads. In *To
Kill a Mockingbird*, instructed by fear, hate multiplies like a
cancer on the town of Maycomb, metastasizing in violence
and injustice. Within the poetry and drama of this riveting
tale also lies a textbook study of fear's logic, a casebook in
which each of fear's five types is illuminated in turn and the
courage to overcome them outlined.

WORRY

At heart, the story is a tragedy, but worry inspires much of
its comedy, especially with regard to a haunted house and
the spooky family lurking within. The Radley place, two
doors down from the Fitch home, rivets Scout's imagination
and that of her elder brother, Jem. Together with their summer friend, a boy named Dill, the three children magnify
every rumor about the house with their fevered speculation.
They are not alone in equipping the "phantom of Radley
Place" with fangs and a taste for children's flesh. No child in
Maycomb will eat the nuts that fall into the school yard
from a pecan tree on the Radley property for fear that they
have been poisoned.

The local children christen the phantom himself (whose
real name is Arthur) "Boo," short for "Boogie man." Jem
imagines him as follows:

> Boo was about six-and-a-half feet tall, judging from his
> tracks; he dined on raw squirrels and any cats he could
> catch, that's why his hands were blood-stained—if you
> ate an animal raw, you could never wash the blood

off. There was a long jagged scar that ran across his face; what teeth he had were yellow and rotten; his eyes popped, and he drooled most of the time.

Worry doesn't fabricate danger completely; it takes real danger and free-associates. The little truth actually known about Arthur is indeed frightening. Years before, as an adolescent, he stabbed his mother in the leg with a pair of scissors. From that day forward, his austere, uncommunicative father has locked him indoors. The house itself is decrepit and shuttered, and it too presents real dangers.

Even as he haunts them, the three playmates haunt Arthur by acting out his story in their front yard. But as they grow older, his specter and their interest diminish. Perhaps Boo isn't all that frightening after all. Maybe he is harmless, a simple introvert who likes to keep to himself. Their attitude softens further when they suspect that he might be the source of several wonderful gifts (chewing gum, Indian head pennies, and tiny likenesses of Scout and Jem delicately carved out of soap). Might Arthur Radley be the one who has left these gifts in plain sight in the knothole of a tree between their yards? It appears so. Over time—as fear's embers do when left unfanned—the terror Arthur once inspired cools completely, until at last the children walk past the Radley place on their way to school without paying it any mind at all.

INSECURITY

Insecurity is personified in Dill, a boastful child who is always quicker to dare Jem into action than to act himself. In fact, compensating for his insecurities with bluster, Dill could serve as a poster child for emotional fear. When caught off guard by his new friends' innocent questioning, at first he doesn't speak of his family background. He is too ashamed to admit who he is (a fatherless child). To compensate for his felt inadequacy, Dill is soon driven by insecurity to confect, and later freely to elaborate on, an impressive personal biography.

More pernicious, for being fully grown, is the emotional fear powering the bigotry that sweeps through Maycomb during the weeks leading up to Tom's trial. Here appearance and reality are tragically at odds. Driven by the ultimate social defense mechanism—whereby insecurity is compensated for by the accidental advantage of being white—bigotry ropes off and demonizes "the other" in a twisted act of self-protection. Even to those who wear it, hate's true face is veiled beneath the conventions of polite society. If young children are less immune to virtue's pretense than they will be as they grow older, such conventions confuse them nonetheless. To Scout's untutored eye, there is nothing polite about polite society. As she narrates the unfolding drama, her childlike logic and trust are confounded time and again by the way the world works. She comes to appreciate her father's principled valiance, even as she learns to mistrust the piety of anyone in whom fear inspires hatred.

FRIGHT

Despite the overwhelming evidence that Atticus presents to acquit his client, a twelve-man jury unanimously votes to convict Tom Robinson, imposing the death penalty. In the wake of this blatant miscarriage of justice, Tom's accuser, Bob Ewell, a violent and malevolent man, vows revenge on Atticus for embarrassing him publicly in court. Too cowardly to confront Atticus directly, Ewell stalks Scout and Jem, finally jumping them on a dark path between their school and home on the night of the town play.

As it does at appropriate junctures elsewhere throughout the story—when Atticus confronts a lynch mob, for instance, or shoots a rabid dog—the fear instinct kicks in right before Scout and Jem are assaulted. "Run, Scout! Run!" Jem screams as Ewell jumps from behind a tree and grabs the back of his sister's costume. The costume, a chicken-wire contraption meant to represent a ham, saves Scout from harm, perhaps even from death, as several knife holes later hauntingly suggest. Jem is not as lucky and is knocked unconscious, his arm shattered. Before Scout, half smothered and fully blinded within her costume, can make sense of what has happened, she finds herself befriended by a strange man. He leads her down the street toward home, cradling Jem in his arms.

DREAD

Jem's savior is none other than Arthur Radley, whose life at last comes into focus. As spectral as the children had imagined—hollow cheeks, colorless eyes, his hair "dead and thin"—Arthur stays only long enough to assure himself that Jem is all right. Unaccustomed to both company and light, "in the voice of a child afraid of the dark," he whispers to Scout, "Will you take me home?" She leads him up the once forbidding steps of the Radley place. Upon reaching the door, he gently releases her hand. She never sees him again.

Arthur Radley is terrified of life, his very soul possessed by dread. The only world outside his room is the quarter block visible through the slats of his shutters, into which, on occasion, three children stray, acting out his life story to pass the time on long summer afternoons. When he hears a familiar voice cry for help that dark night, overcoming a lifetime of inertia and depression, he picks up his whittling knife, rushes onto the path, and strikes down the monster who is about to take Jem's life. There are millions of ways to defy fear's instructions: this is one of them.

GUILT

One evening Atticus tells his children the story of one of his clients, old Mrs. Dubose, who has just died. They have known her as the vicious creature who assailed them with insults whenever they passed by her front porch. When Jem retaliates by tearing the blooms off her azalea bushes, Atticus forces him to read to her, a harrowing experience. What Jem hadn't known is that Mrs. Dubose had been a morphine addict, struggling to free herself from her addiction.

"You mean that's what her fits were," Jem asks his father.

"Yes, that's what they were. Most of the time you were reading to her I doubt if she heard a word you said."

"Did she die free?"

"As the mountain air," Atticus replies. "I wanted you to see what real courage is, instead of getting the idea that courage is a man with a gun in his hand. It's when you know you're licked before you begin but you begin anyway and you see it through no matter what. You rarely win, but sometimes you do. Mrs. Dubose won, all ninety-eight pounds of her. According to her views, she died beholden to nothing and nobody. She was the bravest person I ever knew." By naming and staring down the source of her guilt, she overcame it.

The best way to avoid guilt in the first place is to give it no cause. To his daughter, Atticus explains: "Tom Robinson's case is something that goes to the essence of a man's conscience—

Scout, I couldn't go to church and worship God if I didn't try
to help that man. . . . Before I can live with other folks I've
got to live with myself. The one thing that doesn't abide by
majority rule is a person's conscience." When Scout gets into
a fight to defend the family name, her father assures her that
no defense is necessary. A clear conscience requires no special protection. To be who you are and do what you can is all
that conscience demands. Tom Robinson's tragedy unfolds
in step with Scout's and Jem's moral education.

After Jem's near-death drama, Scout sits late into the evening with her father in his den. "Atticus, I wasn't scared,"
she assures him. Atticus Finch simply lifts his eyebrows.
When she goes on to claim that "nothin's real scary except in
books," he opens his mouth to reply and then closes it again.
She may have persuaded herself that what she has said is a
very grown-up thing to say, but Atticus knows better. He
knows real fear more intimately than almost anyone. How
can he not? After all, as Scout herself could tell you, her father is the bravest man in town.

Robinson Crusoe

Daniel Defoe

The first English novel has an Everyman as its hero, literature's most memorable story, and the straight-shooting prose of a crackerjack journalist. Together, these elements have ensured its enduring popularity with four centuries of readers of all ages. Daniel Defoe's *Robinson Crusoe* is also an extended meditation on courage.

In many ways, the author himself is a profile in courage. A bit of knowledge about his personal story is useful background for the book. Defoe knew fear's acquaintance intimately. At an early age, as a high-rolling importer of spices from the South China Sea, he got himself so deeply into debt that he never could dig out of it. Keeping his guilt alive, despite later becoming among the most prolific writers in history, Defoe spent his entire life eluding the law. Nor would he ever fully recover from the shame of having lost his wife's handsome dowry and the subsequent agony of failing to provide a secure living for her and their seven children.

Not only did Daniel Defoe know the combined fear of

conscience, creditors, and bankruptcy court, but his religious convictions and their bold expression in pamphlets addressing the thorniest issues of the day landed him in jail as
well, once for a month in the dreaded Newgate prison. When
sentenced to public humiliation in the stocks, he penned a
"Hymn to the Pillory," satirizing his judicial and clerical enemies by name. In appreciation of his wit and boldness, for
three days the people of London threw flowers rather than
greet him with the brickbats that crowds customarily hurled
at prisoners consigned to the stocks. Nevertheless, he won
no favors on either side of the religious divide he attempted
to bridge.

Extending his acquaintance with fear, to supplement his
patchy income from journalism and advance his ideals, Defoe risked his life dozens of times during several terms of
duty as one of most successful undercover agents in the history of the royal secret service.

Defoe explores the nature of fear in each of his novels, but
nowhere more brilliantly than in *Robinson Crusoe*. We all
know the story. Washed up on the beach of a desert island,
the book's hero and namesake awakens to discover himself
the sole survivor of a shipwreck. He survives by wanting
what he has, doing what he can, and being who he is.

WANTING WHAT WE HAVE

Paralyzed by fear, Crusoe at first can do nothing but conjure
up images of the many necessities for survival that he lacks:
"Food, House, Clothes, Weapon, or Place to fly to." Then he
does something that (as I suggest above) we ourselves might
try more often. To compose his mind, he draws up a mental
list, contrasting things he lacks with those for which he can
be grateful. Beginning with the "evil" of being "cast upon a

horrible desolate Island, void of all hope of Recovery," Robinson Crusoe answers this grim reality by reminding himself, "But I am alive, and not drown'd as all my Ship's Company was." In this same spirit, the list continues. On one side of his inventory, he reflects that "I have not Clothes to cover me," countering it with "But I am in a hot Climate, where if I had Clothes I could hardly wear them." He finds himself "banish'd from humane Society," but he is "not starv'd and perishing on a barren Place, affording no Sustenance."

On the second anniversary of his shipwreck, with no greater hope of deliverance than before, Crusoe spends "the whole Day in humble and thankful Acknowledgments of the many wonderful Mercies which my Solitary Condition was attended with, and without which it might have been infinitely more miserable." He wants what he has.

DOING WHAT WE CAN

We can almost read *Robinson Crusoe* as an instruction manual filled with how-to tips on what to do if we should find ourselves stranded in the wilderness. First, he forages through the wrecked ship's stores for essential tools and even the occasional luxury. He builds a lean-to, which soon he develops into an impregnable fortress. He digs a well, fashions fishing equipment, and carves out a shelf in the rock to keep his powder dry. He explores the island, secures his safety against wild animals, and invents dozens of other ways to master his environment. Accomplishing the things that fall within his power—however limited it may seem—fills his every waking hour. Soon he is developing agriculture on the island, expanding his stores, raising goats, and achieving self-sufficiency. He does what he can.

BEING WHO WE ARE

Most impressively—and this turns out to be a years-long project—Robinson Crusoe embraces who he is. No longer does he have any reason to be crippled by comparison. With his life stripped of all superficial markings—all those badges of education, status, and success that distinguish one person from another in the hierarchy of society—he taps and draws strength from his innate reservoir of faith and courage. The very things necessary for him to survive prove sufficient for him to prosper.

Perhaps the growth of the spirit can be revealed on a desert island more perfectly than where perverted by society's expectations and competitive games. Yet by stripping life bare, the author makes a point that we forget too quickly in all our strivings. Comparison gives us no insight into our essential selves. As for our existential selves, health and ingenuity—coupled with nature's bounty and, finally, the gift of a boon companion—constitute life's fundamental requirements. Security is not so much overrated, Defoe seems to say, as miscalculated and therefore misunderstood.

FEAR ITSELF

More than a few critics deem it the most frightening moment in the annals of fiction—Robinson Crusoe's discovery of a man's naked footprint in the sand. The revelation that (instead of being alone on his island) he has company shakes him to his very core. Bereft of his sense of security (which he now has reason to believe was an illusion all along), he panics. Should he root up his cornfields to avoid detection, free his goats, never again light a fire, tear down his residence and return to the trees? "O what ridiculous

Resolution Men take when possess'd with Fear!" Crusoe later reflects. "It deprives them of the Use of those Means which Reason offers for their Relief. . . . The Frights I had been in about these Savage Wretches, and the Concern I had been in for my own Preservation, had taken off the Edge of my Invention for my own Conveniences."

For weeks Crusoe succumbs to the prompting of a fevered imagination, never once leaving his cave, unable to pray, a prisoner to his fears. He whips himself into a phobic state, indistinguishable in its symptoms from constant fright. The agitation of his thoughts "set my very Blood into a Ferment, and my Pulse beat as high as if I had been in a Feaver, meerly with the extraordinary Fervour of my Mind about it." Nostalgia for the peace he enjoyed before that fateful day when he encountered the footprint leaves him longing for a release from "the Life of Anxiety, Fear and Care" that now possesses his soul.

The actual danger is no different from before. All that has changed is that Crusoe is now conscious of it. "I had walk'd about in the greatest Security, and with all possible Tranquillity; even when perhaps nothing but a Brow of a Hill, a great Tree, or the casual Approach of Night, had been between me and the worst kind of Destruction." So it is for each of us, every day we live. Destruction looms just around the corner. To obsess over it does nothing to diminish the danger of death. Instead, it diminishes our pleasure in life.

Finally, Robinson Crusoe begins "to take Courage, and to peep abroad again." Slowly regaining his equilibrium, he recognizes where the true danger lays. He has placed himself at greater risk than have his imagined enemies. To protect his life, he has been destroying it. "It was Self-preservation in the highest Degree," he finally concludes, "to deliver my self from this Death of a Life." Battling his fears, he acts in his own defense, as much as if enemies were actually assaulting him.

Robinson Crusoe wins this battle. By resisting fear's delusion, he neutralizes its power, anticipating Franklin Roosevelt's redemptive insight. "Fear of Danger," he concludes, "is ten thousand Times more terrifying than Danger it self, when apparent to the Eyes; and we find the Burthen of Anxiety greater by much, than the Evil which we are anxious about." Though no longer alone on his island, Robinson Crusoe relearns the lesson that experience taught him when he first arrived there: the only thing he has to fear is fear itself.

Danger also discloses opportunity. One thing his unwelcome visitors bring with them is the eventual means for Crusoe's escape. They also provide him with his cherished companion, Friday, whom he rescues from death and who rescues him, in turn, from solitude. Though years pass between the moment he sees a naked footprint in the sand and the day he sails for home, Crusoe ultimately employs the same thoughtfulness and patience to effect his escape as he had during his first years on the island to secure his livelihood. By the end of his twenty-eight-year adventure as a survivor, Robinson Crusoe has become master of himself and much of what he surveys.

Everyman is the hero of Defoe's masterpiece. We have no difficulty projecting ourselves into the shipwrecked sailor's shoes. That Robinson Crusoe should manage to achieve so considerable a measure of freedom in such terrifying circumstances represents not only an individual accomplishment but a major triumph of the human spirit, one available to all of us.

Not only is Robinson Crusoe Everyman, but he sees himself as such: "I have been in all my Circumstances a *Memento* to those who are touch'd with the general Plague of Mankind, whence, for ought I know, one half of their

Miseries flow; I mean, that of not being satisfy'd with the Station wherein God and Nature has plac'd them." Folly may have impelled him on the journey leading to his shipwreck on a desert island, but courage finds him there. Every reader can take heart, which was Defoe's idea in the first place. After all, if Robinson Crusoe can free himself from fear, by wanting what we have, doing what we can, and being who we are, surely so can we.

The Little Prince

Antoine De Saint-Exupéry

It cannot help but make us wonder how an individual whose life so completely embodied the courage to act managed to write his masterpiece on the courage to love and the courage to be. Antoine de Saint-Exupéry won renown in the early years of flight—risking his life in midnight mail runs over the Andes, living to tell of crash landings in the Sahara Desert and at sea, finally to die in a reconnaissance flight over southern France in 1944. An adventure writer, his books model raw courage and gained him international respect as a philosopher of action. He wrote *The Little Prince* (a meditation on love, death, and meaning) the year before his final mission. A fable that can be enjoyed on many levels, it has beguiled readers of every age from the moment it was published.

The Little Prince has best been described as a "cosmic urchin." He leaves his asteroid on a quest for meaning, visiting five other worlds before arriving on Earth, where he makes the acquaintance of an aviator whose plane has gone down in the middle of the desert. A holy innocent, the

Little Prince is constantly bewildered by the "adult" world he encounters on each of the planets he visits.

The Little Prince explores the courage to be as the two companions attempt to survive the harsh desert conditions. And the Little Prince's moral education inspires both him and his student, the pilot, with the courage to love. Earlier in his journey he has learned love's secret from a fox. He teaches this secret to his new friend (and our narrator) before returning home. Among the ways this enchanting book can be read is by unlocking its meaning with my ten keys to freedom.

LIGHTENING UP

Both literally and figuratively, the Little Prince personifies lightness of being. In contrast, the characters he encounters on his journey through space—each a recognizable human type—take themselves with nothing if not the greatest seriousness. He describes one red-faced man who has never smelled a flower, looked at a star, or loved anyone: "He's never done anything except add up numbers," all day long repeating to himself, "I'm a serious man! I'm a serious man!" He is not, the Little Prince insists. "He's a mushroom!"

One asteroid is ruled by a king who has no subjects, another, by a man needy for admirers, who is also the sole occupant of the world he inhabits. The Little Prince encounters a businessman who spends all his time worrying about his money, and a scholar who knows everything but does nothing. The only person he encounters who touches his heart is a lamplighter. "He's the only one who doesn't strike me as ridiculous," the Little Prince says. "Perhaps it's because he's thinking of something besides himself." But this man too fails to recognize the futility of his existence, living on a planet where there is room only for one. When we take ourselves too seriously, being the most important person in the world, we are alone in it.

PRACTICING THOUGHTFUL WISHING

The Little Prince leaves his asteroid because he is dissatisfied with his life and especially with his companion, a vain, simple, and demanding rose. He wants something better from life, something more. Only after he leaves does he look back, with nostalgia, on what he has lost—her companionship, his responsibility of caring for her, and their mutual, if difficult, love.

The Little Prince didn't think to wish for what he had until he lost it. "In those days I didn't understand anything," he admits later. "I should have judged her according to her actions, not her words. She perfumed my planet and lit up my life. I should never have run away!"

RESETTING OUR ALARMS

Stranded in the middle of the desert without water, the aviator fears he won't survive his ordeal. The Little Prince doesn't seem to appreciate his companion's level of anxiety. Instead, he offers up an apparently irrelevant story about his friend the fox. "He doesn't realize the danger," the aviator says to himself. There he is, about to die, and the Little Prince is prattling on about how good it is "to have had a friend, even if you're going to die."

The Little Prince is thirsty, too, however, and they begin walking in search of a well. After walking for hours through

the night, the Little Prince says, "The desert is beautiful."
The man has to admit that this is true. For a moment he forgets completely about his plight. "You see nothing," he muses.
"You hear nothing. And yet something shines, something
sings in that silence."

To which the Little Prince replies, "What makes the
desert beautiful is that it hides a well somewhere."

POSTING A "NO VACANCY" SIGN

Living on one of the planets that the Little Prince visits is a
drunkard surrounded by his bottles. In his stupor, the tip-
pler sits in silence. Filling himself, the drunkard is empty.
The Little Prince asks him why he drinks. He drinks to forget. To forget what? the Prince asks. He drinks to forget that
he is ashamed. Ashamed of what? the Prince asks. He drinks
to forget that he is ashamed of being a drunkard. His life is
completely vacant.

UNWRAPPING THE PRESENT

When they look up at the stars, travelers see guides, scholars
see problems, businesspeople see the sparkle of gold, other
people see nothing but tiny lights—"All those stars are silent
stars," the Little Prince laments. He goes on to complain to
the pilot that people on Earth can raise five thousand roses
in a single garden and still not find the beauty they seek.

The two share a drink of water. "It did the heart good, like
a present," the man reflects. "When I was a little boy, the
Christmas-tree lights, the music of midnight mass, the ten-
derness of people's smiles made up, in the same way, the
whole radiance of the Christmas present I received." The

Little Prince agrees. We don't find what is right before our eyes, even when what we are seeking can be discovered in a single rose or cup of water. "Eyes are blind," he says. "You have to look with the heart."

TAKING THE STAGE

The desert may seem empty and forbidding, but to the Little Prince and the aviator it is the setting for life-and-death drama and timeless love story.

As the man fixes his plane, the Little Prince teaches him what he has learned over the course of his journey. When we dare to love, we open our hearts to pain. He has learned this from the fox, who describes love as "taming." None of the people who live isolated in their own private worlds will ever experience the pain and gift of love.

Earlier in his travels on Earth, the Little Prince visits a train station. People seem to be forever on the go from one place to another. He asks the railway switchmen if they are ever satisfied, only to learn that they are not. He can see them through the windows of their trains, yawning or sleeping. Only the children, with their noses pressed against the windowpanes, seem to know what they are looking for. They give their heart to a doll, and it becomes precious to them. So precious that they cry if they lose it. When the Little Prince points this out, a switchman responds, "They're lucky."

ACTING ON 60 PERCENT CONVICTIONS

Since we cannot care for (or tame) anything without learning to love it first, the most important decisions we make are decisions to love. Such decisions are not easy. When we give our heart to another, we open it to be broken. Yet when the Prince realizes that he is responsible for his rose and acts on this realization, his life takes on new meaning.

This, too, he learns from the fox, whom he tames and then must leave. The fox weeps. "It's your own fault," the Little Prince tells him. "I never wanted to do you any harm, but you insisted that I tame you." Yet the fox has gotten something of value in exchange for his pain. "I get something," he says mysteriously, "because of the color of the wheat," adding: "Go look at the roses again. You'll understand that yours is the only rose in the world."

REMEMBERING THE SECRET TO IT ALL

We see clearly only with the heart—that is the fox's secret. What makes the Little Prince's rose so important to him is the time he devoted to it—to another. "You become responsible forever for what you've tamed," the fox says. "You're responsible for your rose."

Saint-Exupéry elsewhere says that the secret to being human has a trick to it. "That 'trick' is sacrifice," he writes. "And by sacrifice I mean neither renunciation of all good things of life, nor despair in repentance. By sacrifice I mean a free gift, a gift that demands nothing in return. It is not what you receive that magnifies you, but what you give."

When the Little Prince leaves his planet, he is thinking only about himself. Not until he is half a universe away does he recognize that the meaning of his life pivots on the petulant little rose he had tamed and for which he bears responsibility. To tame is to establish ties. Which means that the rose has tamed him as well. He must stop thinking about himself and find his way home.

PRAYING FOR THE RIGHT MIRACLE

"Grown-ups like numbers," Saint-Exupéry's narrator observes at the outset of his story. "When you tell them about a new friend, they never ask questions about what really matters." We don't inquire about their favorite games or hobbies or what their voice sounds like, but about what they do. Comparison—about money, jobs, the size of our houses—not only breeds insecurity and unhappiness but obscures life's miracles.

The Little Prince wants the man to draw a sheep for him. None of the sheep are quite right, because he can't draw very well. Finally he draws a box and tells the Little Prince that there is a sheep inside. The prince is completely satisfied.

On another occasion, the Little Prince encounters a sales clerk who sells pills that can quench a person's thirst. If we take these pills rather than going to the trouble of drinking water, we can save fifty-three minutes a week. "If I had fifty-three minutes to spend as I liked," the Little Prince says to himself, "I'd walk very slowly toward a water fountain."

LETTING GO FOR DEAR LIFE

Finally the time has come for the Little Prince to return to his planet (or to die, we are not really sure). The aviator, who has repaired his plane, is suddenly aware of "something irreparable" in his heart. He will never see the Little Prince again or hear him laugh. "The important thing is what can't be seen," the Little Prince tells him. As for his laugh, all the man has to do is look up at the stars. They won't be silent. Since he will be up there laughing on one of them, heaven itself will be laughing.

Yet even as the Little Prince tries to ease his friend's pain, he, too, is frightened. A tiny snake curls around his ankle. His body is fading, his life force waning. Wherever he is going, he has to go alone. He weeps. But then he musters up his courage. The Little Prince's final words are "You know . . . my flower . . . I'm responsible for her. And she's so weak! And so naive. She has four ridiculous thorns to defend her against the world. . . . There . . . That's all."

SEVEN FEAR EXPERTS

The Gift of Fear
Gavin de Becker

The Gift of Fear, a collection of stories and lessons by one of the nation's leading experts on crime and violent behavior, is the best single discussion of what I call fright.

For more than twenty years, Gavin de Becker has worked with and learned from leaders in the criminal justice field. His clients include many public figures whose prominence places them in danger. De Becker's expertise grew from more than merely a professional interest. He first learned about the ravages of violence, intimidation, and fear at home. By the age of ten, he had witnessed his mother shoot his abusive father. By thirteen, he had seen his sister assaulted and had endured serious beatings himself. Under these circumstances, he learned to assess dangerous situations. And as he grew older, he learned how to protect himself and those around him from violence. The techniques he developed do not demand unique talents or skills, he says. He simply began with his childhood experiences and let his ghosts become his teachers.

In this time of growing violence, it is essential to recognize that far from being our enemy, fear is instead our ally. Fear is less a beast than a conjurer: "Fear summons powerful predictive resources that tell us what might come next." To free ourselves from unhelpful fear, we must first intelligently employ useful fear to enhance our security.

Violence is not random. In fact, it is quite easily predictable. We need only listen to our fear to develop our predictive capacities. Fear speaks to us in the form of intuition, a detective aide available to everyone if only we might heed it. Intuition born of fear is an organic bodily function similar to breathing or blinking. Like other unconscious processes, our intuition constantly monitors information received through our senses, separating the "merely unusual from the significantly unusual." Intuition seems magical only because we are so used to logical processes that lead us step-by-step toward solutions for our problems. Our intuition's assistance is powerful precisely because it allows us to "journey from A to Z without stopping at any other letter along the way."

Our mind, trained originally by the need to survive, is constantly on the lookout for danger. Even after thousands of years of civilization, it remains wired to protect us from physical harm. For instance, when an alarming news alert flashes across the television, "we watch attentively because our survival requires us to learn about things that may hurt us." Since our brain is attuned to this information and remains on the lookout for danger, our inner voice is trying to tell us something important when it speaks in the language of intuition. Too often, however, we listen to the voice of denial rather than that of intuition. By so doing, we discard crucial information that only fear can offer us.

Not all fear is helpful. When fear lingers, it serves no practical purpose. "Remaining in a state of fear is destructive." Only as we learn to work with fear can we begin to use it selectively and strategically. Conversely, indiscriminate fear can do us harm. "If one feels fear of all people all the time, there is no signal reserved for the times when it's really needed." If we think we are protecting ourselves by staying constantly fearful, we must think again. Fear should be only an occasional visitor. Once we realize that violence is predictable and easily avoided, we also begin to understand how much of the fear we experience is unnecessary. Anxiety, caused by generalized fear and the belief that we cannot predict violence, is—unlike a trained intuition—unproductive. It compounds unnecessary fear.

Duration not only impedes fear's utility but also negatively affects our ability to enjoy life. When fear persists, it turns into worry. True fear is organic; worry is manufactured and almost always destructive. "The relationship between real fear and worry is analogous to the relationship between pain and suffering." The latter half of each equation is destructive and should be avoided whenever possible, whereas the former experience, although unpleasant, is a necessary part of life.

We must discern whether what we fear has the ability truly to harm us. Just as we should use our intuition to heed fear's insight, we can also with great profit pump fear for other useful information that may actually enhance our peace of mind. Fear has many secrets to tell and can be our best counselor, once we learn to ask the right questions. Can my adversary deliver the blow? Is there really a chance I could get hurt? Will I be better off after this experience, even if it promises temporarily to be unpleasant? Such questions, de Becker suggests, can spare us the paralysis of worry (which in turn blunts our fear antennae and therefore makes us less safe).

From Panic to Power

Lucinda Bassett

From Panic to Power touches on every kind of fear (since all are present in anxiety) but devotes particular attention to insecurity and the perfectionism associated with guilt.

Lucinda Bassett opened the Midwest Center for Stress and Anxiety after years of suffering severe panic and anxiety attacks. Her story is a harrowing chronicle of fear's possession. For years, anxiety kept her locked in the house, unable to experience any kind of true connection with her friends and loved ones. She describes how the various symptoms of her anxiety disorder compounded one another, each fear leading to the next, until she felt utterly powerless.

Looking back, she recognizes her anxiety as a gift. Although she describes it as a thief that robbed her of happiness, her struggle against it also taught her to look inside herself for strength. She is a healthy person today because her fears forced her to seek and find inner security. Bassett's message is that however severe our struggles against anxiety may be, we have within ourselves all the security we could hope to possess.

One of fear's most alluring pitfalls is that it encourages us to gorge on unrealistic expectations, which leaves us too full of fantasy to enjoy a healthy dose of reality. Unrealistic objectives can lead to perfectionism, one sure sign that anxiety retains its purchase on our lives. This can be especially difficult for those of us who are used to counteracting anxiety with efficiency and a tightly packed schedule. "Instead of striving for perfection," we should "strive to get comfortable with the fact that things aren't perfect and never will be."

Anyone who wishes to free his or her life from fear must first avoid goals and objectives. Fear can trick us into believing that because we sometimes fail to reach our goals, we deserve to be punished—that we deserve to live an anxious life. Instead of letting anxiety justify our unhappiness, we must instead "cultivate an attitude of forgiveness to ourselves." Forgiveness is fear's mortal enemy. A healthy dose of self-kindness and acceptance can ward off any attack that anxiety may mount against us.

Bassett describes her own anxiety as an emotional disorder, not a mental illness. Her fear was self-created, she believes, and, although she did not recognize it at the time, under her own control. She urges us to challenge our own fears the way she did. The path leading beyond fear lies through a change in attitude. If we change our thinking, we can change our biochemistry, our circumstances, and our lives. Since certain types of thinking encourage anxiety more than others, the solution is to alter our thought processes.

Trusting our own thoughts is difficult, especially for those of us who are mired in the thicket of anxiety. Its allure is powerful, one of the most treacherous things about anxiety being that even though we find it distasteful, we can't let go of it. This is because fearful thoughts help lead us away from deeper concerns that we aren't yet quite ready to confront. As frightening as these concerns may be, it is important to remember that "scary thoughts are . . . only a diversion." If we walk toward them rather than away from them, our feelings of anxiety lessen on their own.

Anxiety debilitates us most when it decreases our capacity for risk. As we become more anxiety-prone, we find it ever more difficult to resist fearful thoughts. Our felt ability to push ourselves to improve diminishes. In the end, if we want success, we must be willing to take risks. "Nothing wonderful comes without risk."

Overcoming fear means risking fearful outcomes. Even as we push past fear, we may fear the results of our efforts. Our own anxiety tries to persuade us that overcoming fear isn't worth the effort. But it is a fool's bargain to give in to the very power that holds us back. "You're going to have pain either way, whether you avoid anxiety or not, so you might as well be in control and know that the pain is bringing you closer to your goal."

Fear may also attempt to convince us that the work entailed will force us to change too many things in our lives, even who we are. We mustn't credit disparaging thoughts such as these. "Feeling better doesn't require that you change your personality completely." In fact, as we struggle against and triumph over our anxieties, certain of our personality traits can be turned into assets. Anxiety isn't going to go away by itself. We have to "take the first step, anxiety and all, and then allow the fear to dissipate."

Laughter can help shore up our confidence. If we find humor in our situation, we may just be able to laugh our way out of it. We must also try to overcome our self-consciousness. As we work our way through fear, we may feel strange, but we don't look strange. Fear may try to persuade us otherwise, but to the rest of the world, we look just fine.

Despite all the messages that our anxiety sends us, nothing can take away our capacity to heal. "Life is a fabulous adventure," Bassett concludes. "It wasn't meant to be lived in fear."

The Answer to How Is Yes

Peter Block

The Answer to How Is Yes examines the courage to act, giving considerable attention to worry and insecurity, especially as they manifest themselves at work.

Peter Block is a successful corporate and organizational consultant. What sets this book apart is his unorthodox approach to overcoming fear in the workplace. *The Answer to How Is Yes* emerged from a dilemma Block faced during his training seminars. People go to such seminars seeking answers to the question "How?" After listening politely, at the end of each session some member of the group always asks Block "how" to implement his suggestions. The need to know how to get from here to there arises from the human desire for control and predictability. In an uncertain world, we move forward confidently only when assured of a predictable outcome. This is especially true in the workplace, which is one reason it is so ridden with fear.

"How" questions, though intended to resolve our fears, instead compound them. The more we insist on knowing "how" before we act, the more authority fear has over us. Under the pretext that we do not have all the proper information or permission, fear can paralyze us from taking action. An apparently commonsense question, "How?" often serves as fear's instrument for maintaining control.

"How?" is therefore the wrong question to ask. We waste our time wondering "How does one do that? How long will it take? How much will it cost?" Such questions reinforce our fear by setting tight boundaries for any action we may permit ourselves to take. By framing our efforts in terms of procedure, time, and cost, we forfeit effectiveness to fear.

Fear plays a particularly destructive role in boss-employee relationships. Block tells the story of one highly respected employee, a self-possessed and confident man, who quivers in his boss's presence. Another holds fifteen coworkers he had invited to a meeting hostage while speaking to his boss, who had called in with a minor problem. Fear literally rules the workplace. If our immediate supervisor doesn't scare us, just move up through the chain of command and someone up there will.

Fear—this kind and many others—is our own creation. We might ask ourselves, "What expectations do I have that lead to fear and caution?" The answer will spring from our feelings of dependency. We believe that our bosses can give us something that we cannot give ourselves. We also recognize that they may punish us no matter what efforts we make to protect ourselves from their reprisal.

To turn a perceived problem into a solution, uncertainty itself is one cure for fear in the workplace. Certitude is impossible, anyway. For instance, contrary to popular belief, it is impossible to know what our boss really thinks about us. However far fear may drive us into the depths of our supervisor's psyche, there is little rhyme or reason for why someone likes or dislikes us. Hiring and firing decisions tend to be based on things we can neither control nor anticipate.

Even should we seek his or her opinion about us, our boss is probably not our best source of feedback. "This is not the aspect of life to be strategic or tactical about." If we hope to lower our fear level by pleasing the boss or doing things that make us liked, we are grasping at straws. "Seeking certainty in human affairs breeds doubt and the belief that we are not enough." Seeking an answer to the question "How?"—craving conclusive evidence and foolproof plans—only increases workplace anxiety. It certainly doesn't embolden us to act resolutely and without fear.

Therefore, we should approach our bosses differently—not fear what they may do, but ask ourselves what their intentions are. Instead of worrying about how our supervisor's decisions may have an impact on our job, we might instead ponder how the business benefits from these decisions and how we may best advance them.

Establishing fearless workplace dynamics is everyone's personal responsibility in his or her role as a "social architect." A social architect is someone who is "concerned with how people are brought together to get their work done and build organizations they want to inhabit." This role requires no technical expertise. "The capacities of the social architect are all around us." In a workplace free of fear, crafting a healthy social space becomes everyone's job. From paying attention to how people are seated around a table to deciding who is included at that meeting, the social architect plays an indispensable role.

By defining the position of the social architect so openly, Block imagines an atmosphere of abundance rather than one of fear. Social architects act in concert with their coworkers to counteract fear's hold on the workplace, a dynamic that makes the old model of fearful employee and demanding boss obsolete. When both employees and supervisors leave fear behind, "we affirm [both] our freedom and our commitment" to the fundamental goals and values of the organization.

In a world in which the foremost symbol of humanity, the heart, can be conceived of as a machinelike "pump," we must reacquaint ourselves with its more mysterious essence. We shouldn't view our life or work as a set of problems to be solved, leading us fearfully to ask the question "How?" "Mystery and imperfection restore our humanity. . . . Our willingness to accept an imperfect, paradoxical world" is directly proportional to our ability to overcome fear.

Block prescribes doubt as a tonic for fear. Rather than offering quick-fix solutions, he lauds freedom and mystery, calling formulaic road maps an assault on them both. To neutralize fear in the workplace, we shouldn't seek to offer the right solutions. We should ask the right questions instead (few of which begin with the word *how*). In Block's view, "If we can accept that there is no solution to human problems, that they cannot be engineered or purchased away, then we can accept that the question is more important than the answer."

Freeing the Soul from Fear

Robert Sardello

Freeing the Soul from Fear, a meditation on the courage to be, explores and confronts the power of dread.

Robert Sardello is cofounder of the worldwide School for Spiritual Psychology and the author of many books on healing, spirituality, and the study of the soul. He has recently dedicated himself to applying the insights of individual psychotherapy to contemporary cultural concerns.

Sardello's most important insight on fear cuts to the heart of how we feel when in its grip. Fear strips away context, identity, and personality from our life. When we are fearful, we lose awareness of the things that make us distinct individuals. We even lose all sense of place, for we are no longer rooted in our present surroundings. Consequently, we lose our self-confidence and sense of identity. We assume an identity projected onto us by someone else. Fear is an aggressor that turns us into a victim.

Fear has become like a god. It is invisible but omnipotent. It is all-powerful and all-knowing, dwarfing anyone who attempts to rise up in resistance. Fear kills the future

by erasing our sense of destiny. Hiding is not an option, because "by hiding in the anonymity of the world we are
adding to the facelessness that feeds the nihilistic imagination" of fear. To counter this trend, we must assert our individual will and proclaim our individual identity. Engaging
our true selves with the world is the only way to respond to
fear.

Bodily reactions to fear, such as panting, sweaty palms,
and an increased heartbeat, are evidence of how fear dis-
rupts our bodies and our senses. More important, fear dis-
rupts our will. It eliminates all but the isolated and
frightening future it wants us to inhabit. "Terror allows no
imagination of possibilities other than increased intensity
of the panic." No matter how we imagine our lives or how
we try to make our circumstances different, fear tries to
counteract those efforts.

What happens when fear wins? If we succumb to fear's
assaults, we risk becoming what Sardello calls our own
"double," adopting this term from Otto Rank, the psycholo-
gist and contemporary of Sigmund Freud. Originally,
philosophers and psychologists considered the double a response to the fear of death. The double was life's last-gasp
effort to "preserve itself by producing an external image of
itself." We create our own double to live on after us. By this
definition, although the double may look and act like us, it
lacks will, imagination, and a soul. It is merely a shadow of
its original.

Today, in the growing battle against fear, the double represents something deeper. Should we find ourselves unre-
sponsive to the presence of suffering in the world, this is due
to the influence of doubling. Such an influence is dangerous. If we allow fear to numb us to others, we risk giving it
legitimacy and power over our lives. One answer is to follow
the path of engagement. We must reacquaint ourselves with

the natural world and be willing to respond to the pain of others. The world is filled with fearful shadows of true human beings. If we don't act to temper fear's power, we risk sacrificing ourselves completely to it.

Our bodies play a role in the way we imagine fear, too. Take, for example, the fear of suffering, which frightens us today as much as death frightened our forebears. "We may not be afraid of death [but] we are terrified of what might precede it." Suffering has replaced death at the heart of our fears.

Sardello urges us to recognize the place of the soul in the experience of suffering. The soul, too, expresses itself in our pain. "How we bear our pain may have a great deal to do with what kind of soul work we have done during our life."

Though suffering does not damage the soul, fear can and will if we don't counter its power directly. When fear controls our lives, we make decisions we would not normally make and view ourselves in ways we would not normally tolerate. Many of the strategies we use to ratchet down our fear—weapons, alarms, and worry—don't work. Instead, they "increase the fear they intend to remove."

"Fear is a shape shifter. When we think we have freed ourselves from it, it shows up in the very means we are using to control it." However much we lose touch, however, there is always a path to reconnection; we can always counteract fear through creativity. Fear's undoing is that even when it seeks to destroy, it sparks creativity. For this reason, our most powerful response to fear can be found in artistic beauty. Whether in movement, song, painting, or sculpture, we bring love into the world through beauty and "counter the pervading influence of fear."

It is important not to underestimate fear. We encounter it everywhere. All of us are subjected to its harmful influences daily. Fear is elusive because it hides itself brilliantly within the workings of our mind. "Fear thus becomes insinuated in the very structure of thought, memory, and perception." We must therefore harness our greatest creative forces to counteract it. We cannot destroy fear, but we can neutralize it; we can aspire to create beauty. By so doing, we counteract fear through connection, relationship, and unity.

Sardello invites us to employ meditation and visualization exercises to deepen our ability to counteract fear with creativity. He urges us to seek out beauty in the world and to cultivate it in others. As long as we continue to develop, exercise, and hone the imagination, we strengthen our inner life, our self-identity, and our ability to withstand fear's power.

Embracing Fear

Thom Rutledge

Embracing Fear presents a strategy for courage based on working *with* our fears rather than *against* them.

Thom Rutledge, a well-known psychotherapist, begins his book with an appreciation of Franklin Delano Roosevelt's Four Freedoms address. He then draws from his own practice to illustrate the pitfalls fear places before us. But his observations are more than professional. To supplement the insights he has gleaned from his practice, he adds lessons he has learned from his own successful struggle against fear in his recovery from alcoholism.

We must not work to abolish fear, which is impossible, but develop instead an ability to discern between healthy and unhealthy fear. "Fear is one of the universal experiences that connect us all as human beings." The difficulty is, "we tend to think of fear as part of the problem rather than part of the solution." Healthy fear can offer guidance, support, wisdom, and encouragement, often when we most need it. But to receive its assistance, we must first stop running away from fear.

To help us embrace fear, Rutledge offers a simple and easily remembered acronym: Face it, Explore it, Accept it, and
Respond to it. The first step is to personify our feelings. Fear
is made more terrifying by being faceless and anonymous.
Treat fear as a person and we will recognize that we have a
variety of ongoing (often unhealthy) relationships with our
fear. Although it may not feel this way, we are not powerless
in these relationships. We can talk back to fear; we can bargain, negotiate, and argue with it. We can face up to our
fears by putting a face on them.

Fear does not grow the closer we get to it. In fact, it
shrinks. Once we have faced our fear, we need to explore it
more fully. To accomplish this, we must learn to discern
fear's many voices. When fear whispers in our ear, we
should listen carefully to discern when it is speaking wisely
and when it is speaking falsely. Once we learn to interpret
and discriminate between fear's voices, we can face it head-
on and reject its unwise advice. Eventually, we shall learn
how to disregard its wiles altogether. "When we can refuse
to abide by the voice of fear, the voice of courage will whisper into our ear."

Once we become more aware of fear's true nature by facing it and exploring it, we must then accept its presence in
our life. Since eliminating fear is impossible, "acceptance
that fear is here whether we like it or not is an essential
step." By accepting fear, we discover that "the goal is not to
live without fear, but to live a life not ruled by fear."

Once we have faced, explored, and accepted fear, it is
time for us to respond to it. Fear stalks us just like a "bully,"
waiting to beat us up and leave us cowering in a corner. To
respond, we must stand our ground and call fear's bluff.
Rutledge acknowledges that in recommending this, he is en-
couraging us to move forward into a place of "confusion."
The bully doesn't run away forever the first time we stand up

to him. Nevertheless, "how we respond to fear determines how effectively we will face and push through the walls in our lives."

One of Rutledge's goals is to dispel what he calls the "myth of singularity." Not only is it impossible to entertain only one opinion at any one moment, but it wouldn't be advisable even if we could. "We have busy committees at work between our ears." Especially when it comes to fear, we must not lapse into "monologic" thinking. Part of accepting fear requires that we accept the natural flow of call and response in our minds.

Fear pulls us away from the present. The more we lose touch with the present, the more likely we are to be consumed by fearful thoughts. In illustration, Rutledge describes a psychotherapy session. In the midst of his comfortable office and the unhurried conversation, there is no danger. In this safe and controlled environment, nothing could possibly exist to make his patients feel afraid. But fear forces its way in nonetheless. Trouble visits when his patients think of things that took place outside his office. To find trouble, we often must travel outside the present moment, leading us to misread our current situation as more threatening than it actually is. Fear arises from our thinking about circumstances that might threaten or diminish us, not from the circumstances themselves.

Feel the Fear and Do It Anyway

Susan Jeffers

The central message in *Feel the Fear and Do It Anyway*, which explores the courage to act, is that no matter what happens to us, "we can handle it!"

In the mid-1980s, Susan Jeffers had it made: a doctorate in psychology, a successful therapeutic practice, and a fulfilling personal life. Yet she was a daily victim of fear. It never seemed to abate and she didn't have a moment's real peace. Instead of moving from one success to another, for years she "hung on to many things in my life that clearly were not working." Her fears became so persuasive that they finally drove her to despair. After many tears and many failed solutions, she reached a turning point and began to unlearn a lifetime of fear.

Learning is the key to overcoming fear. Although it may feel intractable, fear is anything but—we need only learn how to root it out. Fear responds especially well to re-education. We can use our mind like waves lapping against fear to wear it away, dissolving it into sand. Jeffers herself "*unlearned* the thinking that had been keeping me a prisoner of my own insecurities."

Whatever our external circumstances, we have the capacity to make things turn out right. Our self-destructive faith in the opposite belief lies at the center of every one of our fears, whether we fear things that happen to us or things that we do, or whether our fears touch on deeper concerns such as success and disapproval.

Fear is a state of mind. We can control our fears without first having to change the world or accept its guidance, yet fear deludes us into thinking precisely the opposite. We end up looking outside ourselves for signs that it is safe to act. In a telling examination of the relationship between fear and procrastination, Jeffers describes how she once suffered from what she helpfully calls the "when/then game." Until she learned to take charge of her fears, she would always wait to act until the time was right. The problem was, the time was very rarely right; fear left her in the waiting room while life passed her by.

The most important question to ask when beginning our struggle against fear is not "Why?" but "What?" We shouldn't waste our energy attempting to figure out the reasons behind our fears. "Does it really matter where our self-doubts come from?" Even if we do stumble upon the causes, they are often opaque and unclarifying. If we focus our energies on what we want to change in our lives, we can overcome fear of the outside world and succeed in building greater trust in ourselves. The "doing always comes before the fear goes away." We must not let fear prevent us from acting, for often action itself dissolves the fear.

Language is one of the most powerful influences on how we think about fear. Fear shapes both our specific choice of words and also the very way we speak about life and ourselves. We can counter fear simply by monitoring the words we use. Phrases such as "I can't" and "I ought" abet fear. "I will" and "I can" bespeak a more positive, less fear-ridden attitude.

It is important to expand our comfort zone with respect to risk. Developing a greater capacity to learn from risk can be liberating. We should take chances only within reason, of course, not risk life and limb or court needless danger.

We must also consider the consequences of actions that may temporarily help us feel less fearful. For example, coopting the power of others to help beat back our own fears will likely backfire. We should therefore look within ourselves for strength. The secret to handling fear is moving from a position of personal pain to one of personal power. Once we do that, "the fear then becomes irrelevant."

Since fear is our constant companion, we must learn how to live with it and turn its power to our own purposes. It will be there with us even when we craft a healthy and balanced life. However, if we train our sights on many different objectives and spread joy evenly throughout our days, fear no longer monopolizes our attention and holds us back. It becomes just another part of our journey.

Getting a grip on our fear is never easy. "It takes courage to mold your life the way you want it to be." We can take heart, however, in the knowledge that fear often accompanies growth. Growth follows directly upon our taking responsibility for our own fears. Without a sense of responsibility for our feelings, especially our fears, we cannot grow.

Love Is Letting Go of Fear

Gerald G. Jampolsky

Love Is Letting Go of Fear explores the relationship between fear and the courage to love.

In 1975 to all the world Gerald Jampolsky was a skilled psychiatrist with a thriving practice. He was fearless, confident, and successful. This is how his friends, family, and colleagues saw him as he approached midlife. In reality, though, his marriage had just disintegrated, he was sinking deeper into alcoholism, and he had developed chronic health problems, which he traced to his high levels of fear and guilt. Just as he was sinking into despair, Jampolsky discovered *A Course in Miracles*. That book and the series of self-help resources patterned after it are the principal sources for his subsequent journey. As is evident from the wide audience that his book has reached and helped, the utility of Jampolsky's insights into the workings of fear are not restricted to those who embrace these particular spiritual tools.

Fear had been Jampolsky's master, one he had chosen himself. Fear victimizes us by narrowing our choices. When

he chose fear, his fear made decisions for him that elimi-
nated every other possibility. Stuck in a seemingly endless
rut, "I found myself with only one attitude, that of fear and
suspicion." When fear becomes a chronic problem, it can
lead to our total immobilization. Instead of concentrating
on possibility and potential, we focus on "what we believe
cannot be changed: on what is over, or on what has not oc-
curred."

Fear distorted Jampolsky's view of others as well. He suffered from self-described tunnel vision, through which he
was unable to appreciate the people in his life or receive the
gifts they brought to it. He found fault with his friends and
family more quickly than he celebrated them. Fear distorted
his perception, leaving him "isolated, disconnected, sepa-
rate, alone, fragmented, unloved, and unlovable."

Fear colors our view of the present by filtering it through
an unpleasant past. The past has "no validity in the present."
Misplacing our priorities, we steal privileges from the present and give them to an undeserving past. "This results in
our seeing the present with distorted dark-colored glasses."

Jampolsky believes that the only true reality is love,
not fear. According to his understanding, the reality that
we perceive—the mundane world of objects, people, and
movement—is not permanent. Only love is eternal and never-
ending, and thus only love can overcome fear. We can tran-
scend fear by changing our belief system, since we can
perceive only what the mind projects outward. All it takes to
live in the present is focus, effort, and diligence.

Living in the present places us on the path from fear to
peace of mind. Both guilty feelings arising from past experiences and fearful thoughts emerging from future expectations disturb and distract us. Preoccupied with these
troubles, we leave no room for the present and therefore no
room for love.

Imagine our life as a film in progress, with the mind its director. "We are what we believe." The mind projects an internal script onto the world, creating the reality that we experience. Although fear may try to hijack the director's chair and turn the plot of our life-movie in the direction of separation and suspicion, we need not let this happen. "Love directs movies that unite and join."

Interpersonal relations follow the same pattern. We hold ourselves back from living in loving relationships much as we hold ourselves back from living fully in the present. Fearful behaviors, such as aggression or defensiveness, are requests for love, even if they seem like the opposite; successful responses to these behaviors cannot emerge from fear. Seeking to change or correct people leads only to more guilt when we see our efforts fail. By living in the present, we can maintain a single-minded focus on love and acceptance.

We must stop taking our failures to heart more completely than we do our successes. Otherwise, we cede ever more control to fear. To counter this tendency, we must practice forgiveness, beginning with ourselves, by abandoning words that bind us to a fearful future and guilty past. Again, words such as *impossible, can't, limitation*, and *shouldn't* are emblems of fear's logic. By learning to employ a healthier vocabulary, we can change our reality.

Each person's struggle with fear must not be viewed only in narrow, individualistic terms. The world is off-kilter. We languish together inside a dysfunctional belief system. "The law of the world states that what we give away, we lose." This attitude could not be more mistaken. Instead of living in fear of scarcity, we must encourage a belief in abundance.

Jampolsky traces his own turn away from fear and toward love to the realization that giving more does not mean having less. "All I give is given to myself," he says. Change must start at the individual level, but as more individuals begin to perceive the world differently and turn away from fear, together we will begin to heal the world with love and compassion.

FREEDOM FROM FEAR

STUDY GUIDE

Questions for Personal Reflection
or Book Group Discussion

The moment we recognize our tears in another's eyes, they no longer blind us. This is one of the things that makes book clubs and study circles so beneficial—when we gather, we receive not only inspiration but also comfort from one another. The most memorable learning is shared learning. *Freedom from Fear* lends itself naturally to this purpose. A group of friends or book-club members, a workplace continuing-education training team, or a spiritual study circle will find it easy to take up a section or chapter at a time for group discussion.

As guides to reflection, you might ponder the following questions as you move through the book or after you have finished reading it. Each is designed to serve a double purpose—either as a topic for personal meditation or, if you are reading *Freedom from Fear* as part of a group, as a springboard for discussion.

Choosing Your Fear. I identify five types of fear: fright, worry, guilt, insecurity, and dread. If you could rid your life of one of these fears, which would it be? Why?

Catching a Fear. Can you remember a time as a child (or more recently) when you "caught" someone else's fear? What happened? What were you afraid of?

A Fearless Life. There is a rare genetic condition that causes people to be born without a sense of touch. Others, who have had the fear-sensing amygdala in their brain damaged, do not feel fear at all. Would you want to be born without a sense of fear? What do you think this would be like? What would be the benefits to a fearless life? And what would be the drawbacks?

Inspiring Courage. Historians have recorded how people all across America were given new hope when President Roosevelt announced to the country that "the only thing we have to fear is fear itself." Take five minutes and imagine that you are a journalist writing the morning headline summing up an inspiring speech that would help you overcome your own biggest fear right now.

An Unlikely Hero. In some ways, raised in privilege, FDR was an unlikely figure to rise onto the ramparts and vanquish fear. Think of people in your own life—friends or family members perhaps—who are also unlikely profiles in courage. What did they do to overcome fear? What challenges did they face? What can you learn from them?

False Alarms. Can you remember an instance in which you experienced false alarm? Have you subsequently taken any action to make sure you wouldn't get fooled in the same way again? What did you do? Some fears have short shelf lives, like a child's fear of the dark. Can you think of a fear from your childhood that is no longer part of your life now?

Drawing a Courage Lifeline. On a piece of paper draw a line across the page representing your life up until the present moment. Move the line up and down on the page according to how courageous you felt from one period to the next. What gives you courage? What takes it away?

Courageous Performances. Imagine our life story as a movie, complete with character development, sudden plot twists, and an emerging theme. If your life were going to be made into a movie, who would play the lead role? Why would they be perfect for the part?

60 Percent Convictions. Think of a time when you acted on 60 Percent Convictions. And then think of another when you didn't act (because of your 40 Percent Fears). What were the circumstances? In the end, did your decision turn out to be good or bad?

Turning Lemons into Lemonade. One story from *The House at Pooh Corner* describes how Eeyore made the best of a bad situation at his birthday party. Can you think of a time when you turned disappointment into joy? What did it take to make you appreciate your gifts like Eeyore appreciated his broken balloon and empty honey jar?

Making a List. I am a big fan of lists. My favorite kind puts things I am thankful for on one side of a page and things that are haunting me on the other side. Make a list of your own along these same lines. What does your list tell you about yourself and your fears?

Your Worry Tree. If you had a worry tree, what worries would you hang on its branches? Can you imagine them not being there in the morning when you return to pick them up?

Fear and Knowledge. Robinson Crusoe was surprised by his fearful reaction after seeing the footprint in the sand on his deserted island. Do you think he was better off before or after learning he was in danger?

Your Ethical Will. Take ten minutes and write your own ethical will. Be sure to make a list of "life lessons" like the one's Michael shared with his children. What would you include in your ethical will? To whom would you address it? Was there anything you wrote down at first but then took off your list? If you had to put one lesson at the top, which would it be?

Who Were We? Write your own brief obituary, limiting yourself to five lines or less. What did you include in your paragraph? What did you consciously find yourself leaving out? If you had to write another paragraph to cover everything from the present moment forward, what would you hope to say about yourself that you couldn't say now?

ACKNOWLEDGMENTS

Fear is one of two topics (along with grief) that I have long wished to have a ready primer for—one I could give to those whom I counsel when they ask what they might read to help them get through a particularly difficult patch. I've always wanted to have at my fingertips a practical, accessible, and encompassing book on fear, something like *Everything You Ever Wanted to Know About Fear But Were Afraid to Ask*. For years I have played with how such a book, if it existed, might be organized—beginning with a clear description of fear, followed by useful tips for overcoming it, all to be supplemented by a broad set of helpful resources, with suggestions for further reading and study.

With this vision in mind, I approached Tim Bent, my editor at St. Martin's Press. Not only is Tim the most talented and demanding editor I have had the privilege to work with, but he is also willing to take chances and encourages me to do the same. Neither of us had done a self-help book before. He jauntily proposed that if Ralph Waldo Emerson were writing today, he would more than likely be considered a self-help author.

This added to my sense of inadequacy as much as it proved an inspiration, but with Tim's encouragement and steady guidance, I charged ahead. To the extent that I have been successful in producing the book I set out to create, a large measure of responsibility for that success is Tim's. Where I may have fallen short reflects, of course, my limitations alone.

When Tim moved to Harcourt from St. Martin's, I confess to experiencing a few of the very fears that I caution against. I should not have been surprised when they proved baseless. My new editor, Julia Pastore, has done a brilliant job shepherding this book through production, for which I am deeply grateful.

The one other person without whose help I could not have written this book is Marc Loustau, my research assistant, who is preparing for the ministry as a student at Harvard Divinity School. Unlike me, Marc is not the least bit daunted by the Internet. Searching there and through the library stacks, he brought me enough interesting and helpful material for a dozen books on fear. In addition, he helped me pull together the *Freedom from Fear* Book Club and worked on the study guide. As kind as he is brilliant, Marc will not only be writing books of his own soon, but, more important, will be a wonderful pastor.

I dedicate this book to my congregation, the great family of All Souls. Looking back over more than a quarter century together, my gratitude for having been called by and to such a splendid congregation knows no bounds.

New York City
All Souls Unitarian Church
Thanksgiving 2003

Forrest Church has served the past quarter century as senior minister of All Souls Unitarian Church in New York City. Educated at Stanford University, Harvard Divinity School, and Harvard University, where he received his Ph.D., he is the author or editor of more than twenty books, including, most recently, *Bringing God Home: A Spiritual Guidebook for the Journey of Your Life* and *The American Creed: A Biography of the Declaration of Independence*, both also published by St. Martin's Press.